AF594431

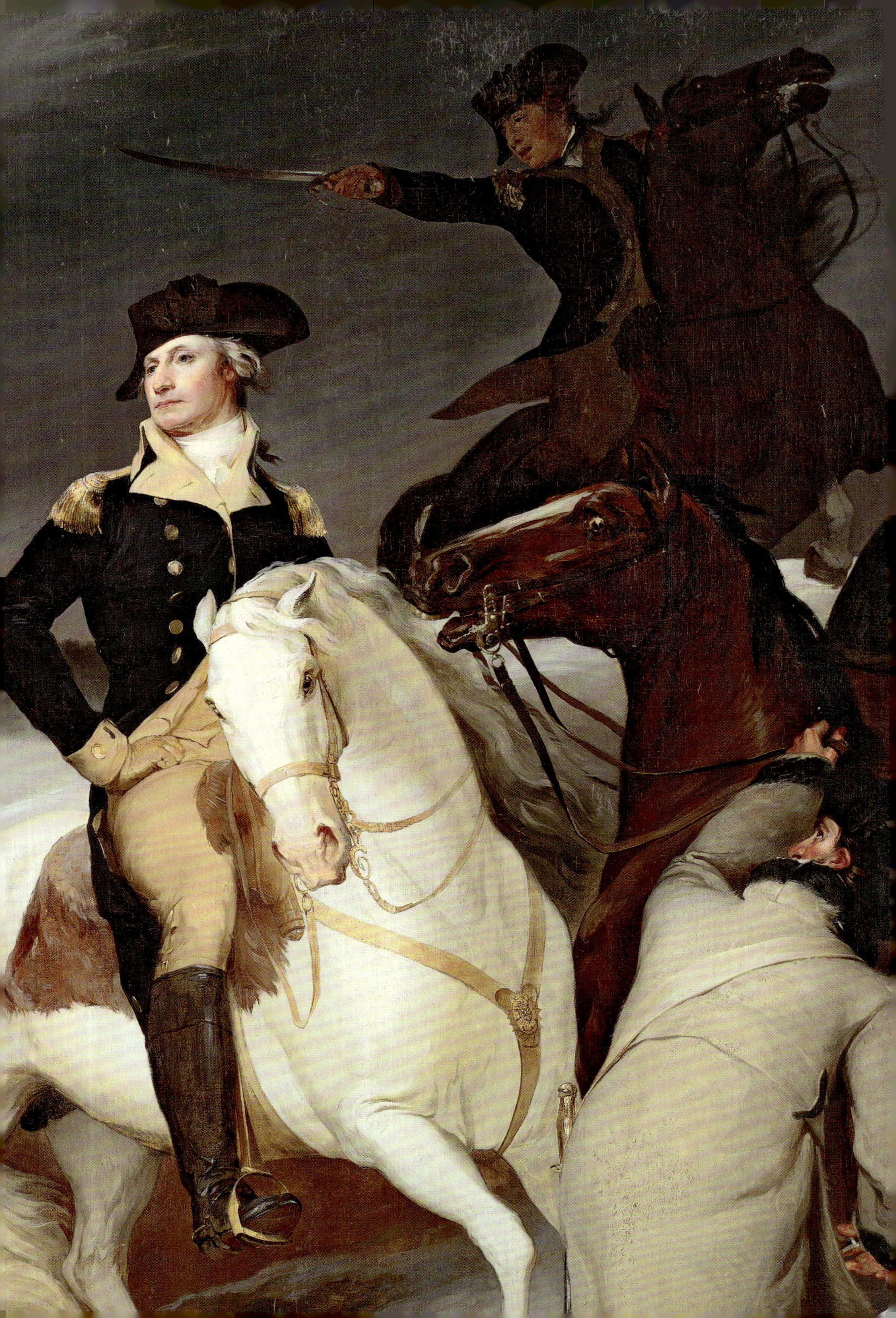

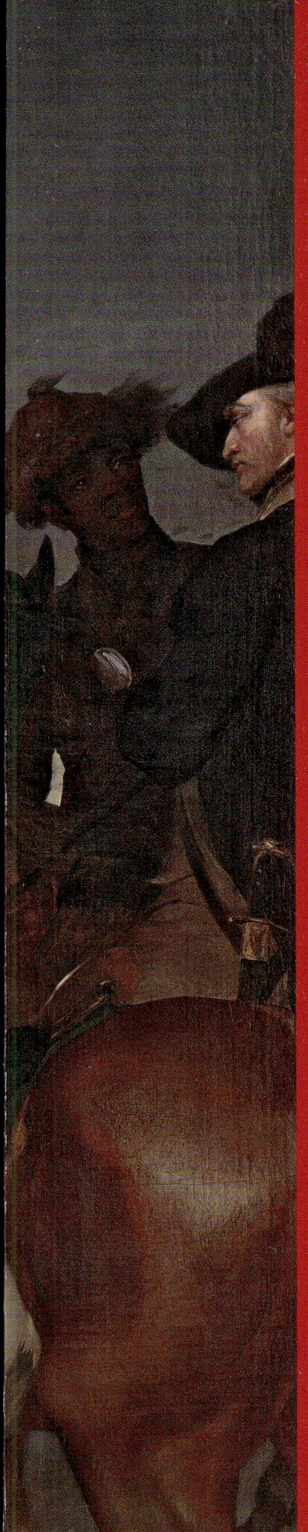

THOMAS SULLY

GEORGE WASHINGTON AND THE PASSAGE OF THE DELAWARE

ELLIOT BOSTWICK DAVIS

MFA PUBLICATIONS | MUSEUM OF FINE ARTS, BOSTON

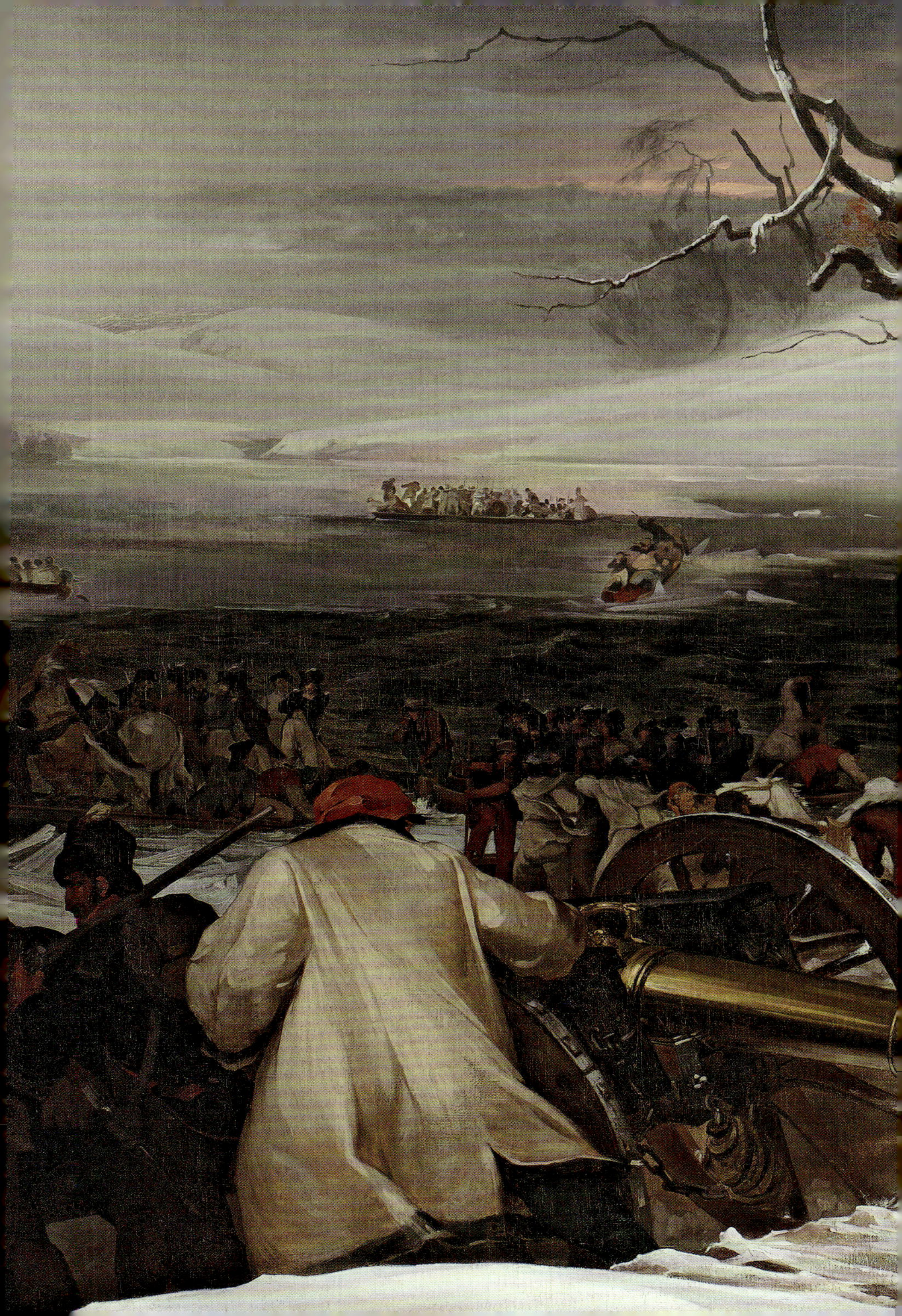

THE PASSAGE OF THE DELAWARE

The Passage of the Delaware transports us to the frozen banks of the Delaware River at a pivotal moment of the American Revolution, on December 25, 1776. General George Washington appears astride his white horse, life-size and brilliantly lit in the center of a massive canvas measuring twelve by seventeen feet. A small cluster of officers and aides, also mounted or preparing to mount, dominates the right half of the composition. Below Washington at left, a soldier with his back to the viewer grasps the handle of a cannon, laboring to steer the gun down a snow-streaked bank. The river is strewn with a confusion of men, guns, and horses rearing from flatboats, as the troops struggle to navigate treacherous ice floes and rapid currents. Through veiled layers of gray and white paint conjuring up the nor'easter storm that shrouded a full moon that night, we are able to see the opposite bank, on the New Jersey side, where snowdrifts nearly bury a tiny shed. Framed within a V-shaped, barren limb, which leads our eye to the distant shore, the rosy glimmers of sunrise break above the horizon.

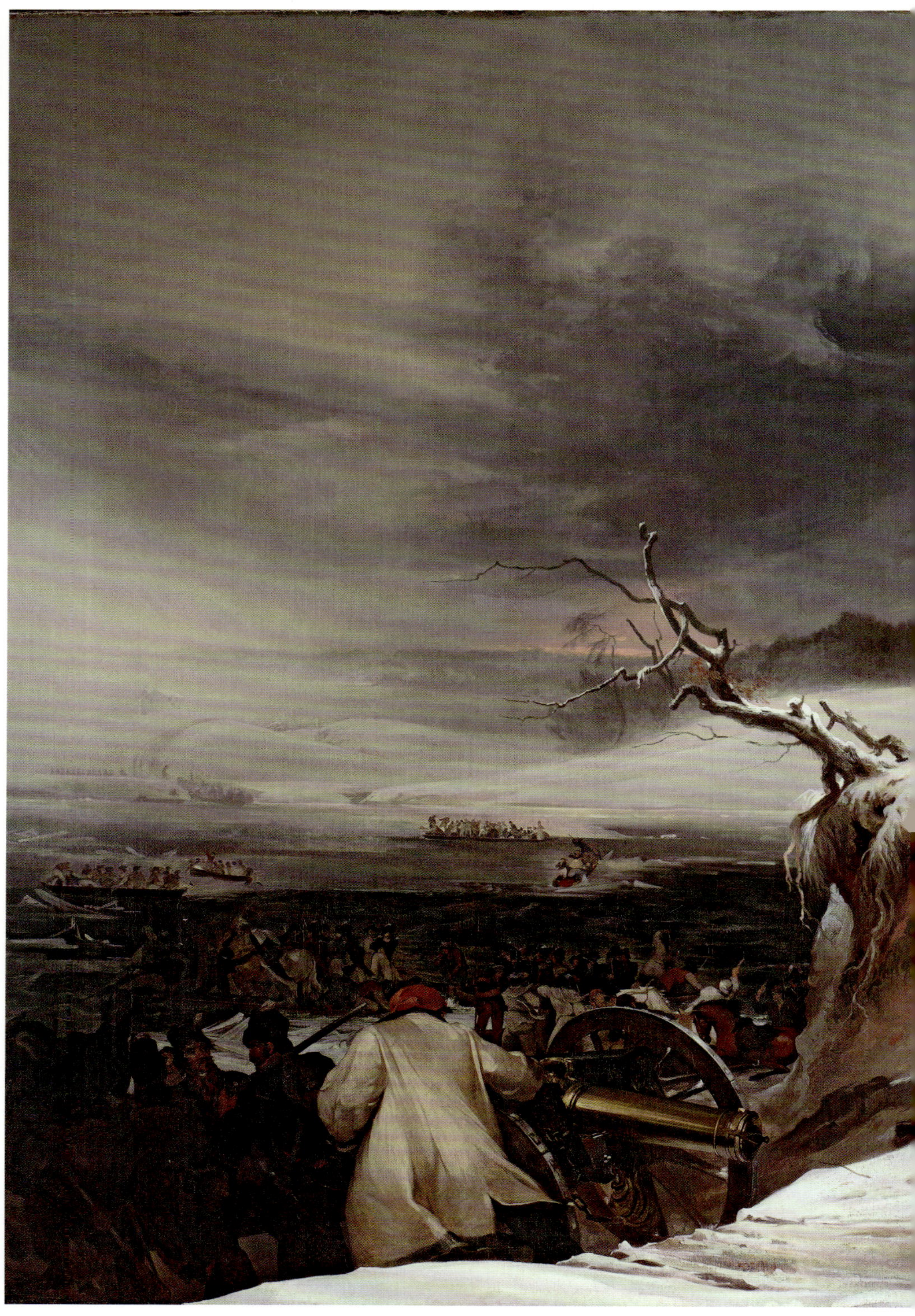

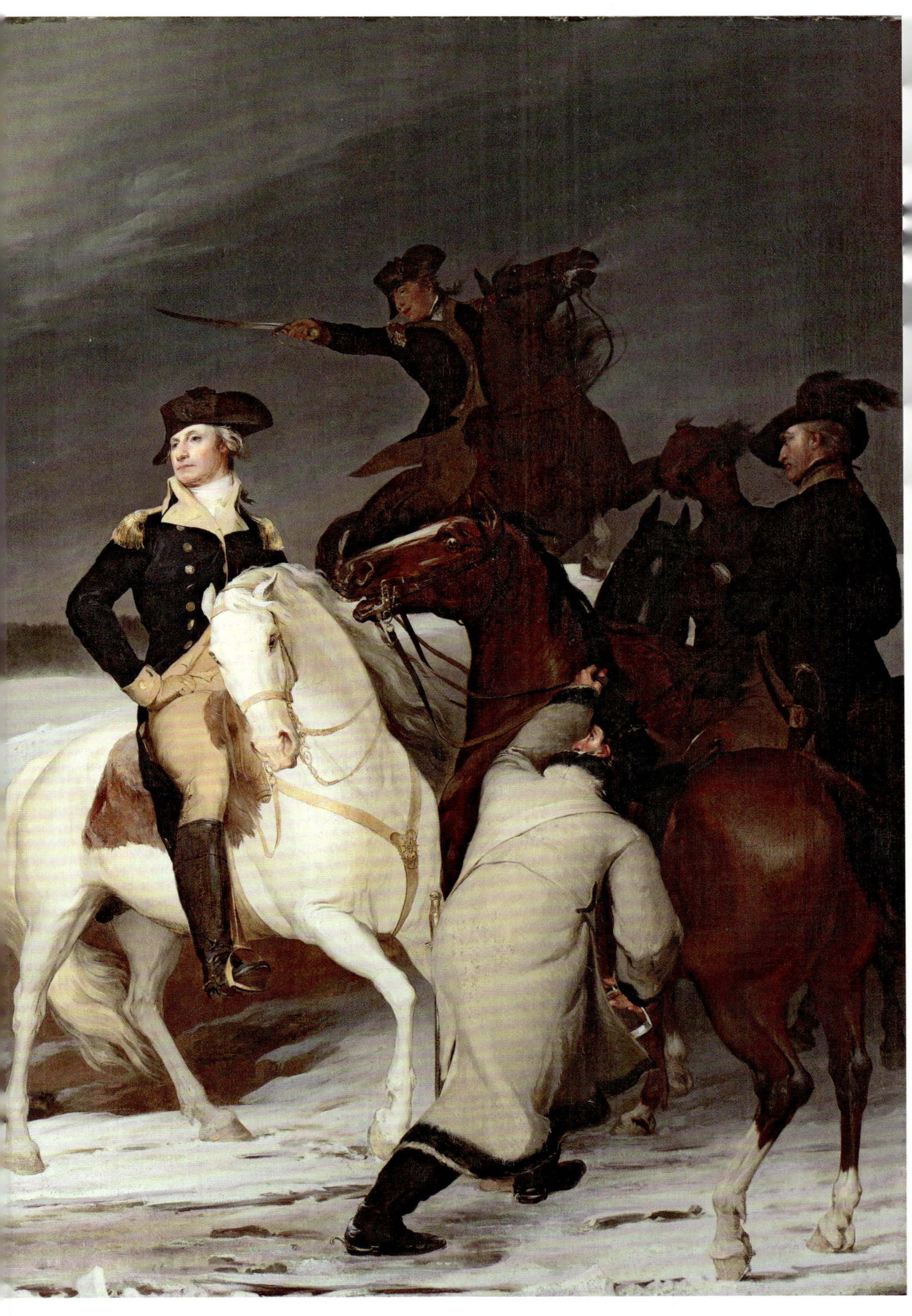

Thomas Sully's painting captures vividly and dramatically a moment in American history when courage and determination turned the tide in the revolutionaries' fight for liberty from British rule. Their password, "Victory or Death," given to the troops to keep their elaborately orchestrated nighttime maneuver secret, signaled high stakes and resolve. In the early days of Washington's command, revolutionary forces amassed at Dorchester Heights caused the British to withdraw from Boston in March 1776. During the months that followed, the Continental Army suffered heavy casualties during the Battle of Long Island and had been forced into a hasty nocturnal retreat from Manhattan—a disappointing setback for Washington, who had hoped to capture New York. By December, Washington was Commander-in-Chief of a rapidly dwindling corps of independent regiments. Soldiers were eager to return home, as their terms of enlistment were set to expire at year's end. Knowing that American and British forces would soon be suspending battle during the winter months, Washington committed 6,500 troops—many in ragged clothing and all but barefoot—to the Trenton operation, to face the far more robust Hessian mercenary forces serving the British Crown. Washington and his officers' bold and courageous tactic was a last resort.[1]

The general planned for what was left of his army to surprise the Hessians at Trenton, by crossing the Delaware River from the Pennsylvania side, west to east. Expected to arrive on the New Jersey bank by midnight, troops would march southeast to Trenton in three flanks, one under Washington's command, and the others led by General James Ewing and Colonel John Cadwalader. Washington chose to cross the river with 2,400 men ten miles north of Trenton, at McConkey's and Johnson's ferries. He would be supported by General Henry Knox, who had been his savior at Dorchester Heights, and by Colonel John Glover and members of his regiment from the seacoast town of Marblehead, Massachusetts, who had ferried Washington and his army across the East River during their clandestine retreat from New York City.

The severe winter conditions that night made the crossing a test of fortitude, according to one participant: "The frost was sharp, the current difficult to stem, the ice increasing, the wind high, and at eleven it began to snow."[2] Unaware that the regiments led by Ewing and Cadwalader were unable to cross the ice-clogged waters at their designated locations, Washington issued orders for his troops to conduct themselves silently to maintain their element of surprise. A full moon that would have aided their navigation was so badly obscured by the storm that Washington instructed the soldiers to follow pieces of white paper attached to the hats of their leaders. In the river, massive ice shards collided, and eyewitness accounts described General Knox commanding the troop and artillery movements with his stentorian bass voice. The New Jersey militia in Hunterdon County had earlier contributed to the army's efforts by scouring the nearby countryside for every flatboat they could find. With the aid of the intrepid seamen of Colonel Glover's regiment and ropes stretched across the water to guide their way against the forceful currents, not a single man, horse, or cannon was lost to the river that night. Landing safely on the opposite shore, the Continental Army marched on to Trenton, arriving just after seven o'clock in the morning, and scored a decisive victory, killing or capturing more than nine hundred Hessian troops.

The dramatic turn of events on Christmas night 1776 inspired visual artists and writers throughout the first half of the nineteenth century. The up-and-coming Thomas Sully produced one of the most compelling scenes of the Delaware crossing in 1819, when faced with his first major public commission, a history painting for the Senate Chamber of the North Carolina State House, in Raleigh. He drew on his own personal experiences and painterly formation, combined with a broad range of artistic models and historical accounts, to forge a new mode of history painting that he called an "historical portrait."[3] Sully's approach, with its distinctive blend of carefully observed details based on historical facts and his own flair for theatricality, captured events from more than forty years earlier in a manner that appealed to viewers of its time and still captivates viewers today.[4]

Born in Horncastle, England, in June 1783—a few months before the American Revolution ended with the Treaty of Paris signed that September—Sully immigrated to the United States with his parents in 1792 and came of age as an artist as the new nation was beginning to find its place on the world's stage. Like other artists, writers, architects, and designers who sought to legitimize the United States and its leaders by associating them with models from the past, Sully cast Washington in the role of *exemplum virtutis*, the example of virtue venerated in ancient Greece and Rome and revived in the Neoclassical period of the early nineteenth century.[5] And yet, in conceiving imagery appropriate for the young republic, Sully ironically turned to portraiture and history paintings celebrating the great empires and monarchies of Europe, such as the one that the Patriots had fought valiantly to overthrow.

At George Washington's funeral in 1799, his fellow Virginian, soldier, and statesman Henry Lee famously proclaimed him "First in war, first in peace, first in the hearts of his countrymen."[6] Washington's reputation was exemplary, yet after completing his second term, he resigned the role of president to return to Mount Vernon. There he chose to live out his life in the manner of the fifth-century BC Roman general and statesman Lucius Quinctius

Cincinnatus, namesake of the Society of the Cincinnati, which was established by officers of the Continental Army and their French counterparts to support revolutionary veterans and their families.[7] Beginning with ceremonies marking his death and leading up to the centennial of his birth in 1832, Washington was increasingly celebrated for his leadership during the eight years of the American Revolution and during eight more as the nation's first president. Washington hagiography peaked around the middle of the nineteenth century, remained strong through the nation's centennial in 1876, and lasted well into the early twentieth century in the later decades of the Colonial Revival. In 1859 the *Home Journal* observed, "In all branches of Art and in all shapes of Literature, Washington is now the leading subject—dwelt upon in essay, oratory and poetry, and represented in engraving, painting, and marble."[8] Sully's monumental image *The Passage of the Delaware* stands as one of the earliest and most innovative expressions of the cult of Washington in the visual arts.

Sully's conception for the painting belongs to a larger cultural effort to proclaim the legitimacy of the young republic to audiences at home and abroad. Public art and architecture have a long history of being used to bestow gravitas on institutions, whether sacred or secular, royal or republican. In the United States, the commemoration of the nation's early history came to the fore after the War of 1812, when the British invaded Washington, D.C., and set fire to the White House and the Capitol building during a conflict that was cast as a second War of Independence. After the war ended, in 1815, cities throughout the nation were quick to name streets and thoroughfares after George Washington and to erect public buildings decorated with imagery meant to inspire the populace to emulate virtuous leaders.

Sully's *Passage of the Delaware* was an early harbinger of

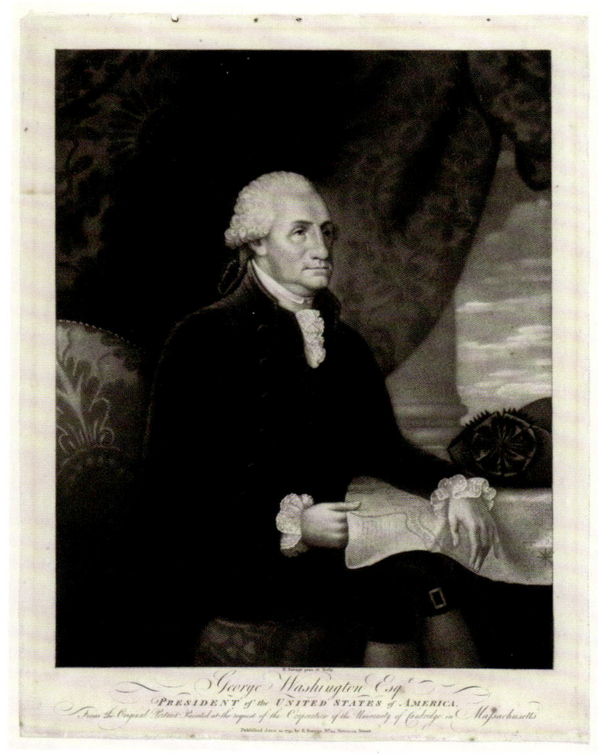

Edward Savage, *George Washington*, 1793

this trend. The majority of monumental scenes portraying Washington during the American Revolution appeared later, beginning in the 1830s, when artists were commissioned to produce a host of sculptures and paintings for the rebuilt United States Capitol. In 1834, Horatio Greenough modeled an enormous statue of Washington, referring to the statue of Zeus at Olympia, that represented the hero bare-chested, cloaked in a toga, and proffering a sword, while seated with a plowshare at his feet. The sculpture was installed in the Capitol rotunda in 1841 and was joined in 1865 by a painting for the rotunda ceiling, *The Apotheosis of Washington*, by Constantino Brumidi, portraying the former president ascending to the heavens wearing a toga beneath his military jacket. But most images of Washington circulated in the United States were less grandiose depictions, and at smaller scales. During the founder's lifetime, popular prints were economical to produce and sell. Also popular were cabinet-sized paintings such as Jacob Eichholtz's *An Incident of the Revolution* (1831, Museum of Fine Arts, Boston), in which Washington's second in command, Major General Charles Lee, wearing tattered civilian dress, is mistaken for a common vagrant.

One of the driving forces in celebrating Washington as a virtuous soldier and statesman during the first decades of the country's existence was the need to solidify a union of disparate states in support of the nation's founding principles, as affirmed in the Declaration of Independence and the Constitution. State politicians seeking to bind their constituents to a national form of government seized upon Washington as a powerful unifying symbol and a worthy model of citizenship. It was in this context that the members of the General Assembly of North Carolina initiated their discussions in January 1800 to honor his life at the North Carolina State House in the capital of Raleigh, just a month after the president's burial at Mount Vernon. The legislators voted to commission two portraits of the founder, democratically proposing that one hang in the Senate Chamber and the other in the House of Commons. Despite this initial outpouring of enthusiasm, the North Carolinians did not act on their resolution until 1816, when they approached two painters based in Philadelphia, Rembrandt Peale and Thomas Sully.

Sully set about the prospect of a public commission to portray George Washington with ambition and zeal. He had struggled to make his way as an artist in a young nation largely without government, church, or private patronage. The youngest of nine children born to parents who were actors, Sully accompanied his family to Richmond, Virginia, when he was nine years old.[9] His uncle, Thomas Wade West, managed theaters in Virginia and South Carolina, and two years after the family's arrival in the United States, Sully debuted onstage as a tumbler along with his older brothers, delighting audiences in Charleston with performances in entertainments such as *Two Hunters and the Milk Maid* and the *Old Soldier*. Sully's father aspired for Thomas to develop a proper profession beyond the stage, however, and, in 1795, secured an apprenticeship at an insurance firm for his twelve-year-old son. According to his biographer William Dunlap, a fellow artist and theatrical performer, "the broker complained to his father that although [Sully] was very industrious in multiplying figures, they were figures of men and women, and that if he took up a piece of paper in the office, he was sure to see a face staring at him; in short, that Tom spoiled all the paper that fell his way, or what he could lay his hands on."[10] Far more interested in becoming an artist than in learning the insurance business, Sully began studying art with the French-born artist Jean Belzons, who was his sister's husband.

By the time he was sixteen, Sully had suffered a violent rupture with Belzons. He left Charleston for Richmond, Virginia, the home of his older brother Lawrence, who was eking out a living as a miniature and device painter.[11] Ensconced in his brother's family—which included five surviving children, of nine—Sully set out as an itinerant portrait painter seeking commissions throughout the Commonwealth. When Lawrence died, in 1804, Sully stepped in to help his sister-in-law Sarah Anne raise her young family, and eventually married his brother's widow. In search of training and opportunity, Sully moved his growing family to various northeastern cities, studying along the way with such established painters as John

Thomas Sully,
Self-Portrait, 1807

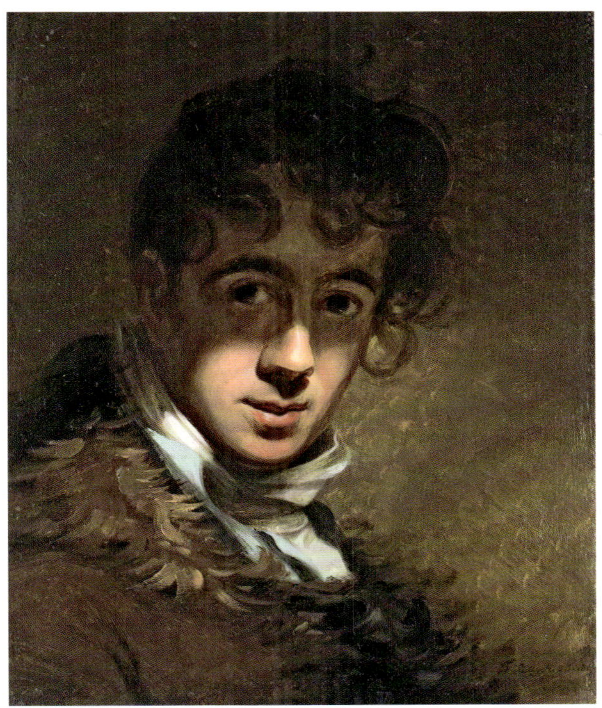

Wesley Jarvis in New York, John Trumbull in Hartford, Connecticut, and Gilbert Stuart in Boston. By 1807, Sully, his wife, and their family had settled permanently in Philadelphia.[12]

Surrounded by the theatrical world from birth, Thomas Sully had witnessed dramatic events enacted on stage and experienced firsthand as a performer how those stories resonated with audiences. His theatrical background may have inspired him to craft in response to the North Carolina commission invitation a new style of history painting that combined dramatic action with accurate portraiture. Early in his artistic career, Sully also demonstrated remarkable entrepreneurial spirit in attracting and expanding his clientele. Rendering likenesses provided steady paid work,

States for large battle scenes, American artists favored panoramic land- or seascapes as the subjects of these large compositions. John Vanderlyn created 165-foot-long paintings of the royal gardens at Versailles (1818–19, Metropolitan Museum of Art), which were later installed in a structure he built in New York to display his work, called the Rotunda.[16] In Boston, John Penniman painted a monumental transparent painting fifteen feet square of the conflagration of the Exchange Coffee House on Court Street, first displayed in 1819, and Robert Salmon produced multiple views of *The British Fleet Forming a Line off Algiers* (1829, Museum of Fine Arts, Boston), several of which still survive at nearly sixteen feet wide.[17] In Philadelphia, at Charles Willson Peale's museum, panoramas of battles at sea were unfurled for the public with accompanying special effects.[18] Thomas Cole's *The Course of Empire* (1836, New-York Historical Society), a series of five large canvases portraying the wilderness as a backdrop to the rise and fall of civilization, made for the private art gallery of the New York collector Luman Reed, was inspired by these earlier popular panoramas.[19]

As a young boy, Sully may well have heard about Boydell's Shakespeare Gallery in London, as well as have seen the folio of engravings issued to fund the picture gallery, whose preface expressed the proprietor John Boydell's hope: "in a country where Historical Painting is still but in its infancy — To advance that art towards maturity and establish an English School of Historical Painting."[20] By the time Sully returned to London as an aspiring artist in 1809–10, supported by his patron Benjamin Chew Wilcocks and four other sponsors, Boydell's gallery was already closed and the collections dispersed. While in London, the prominent American expatriate painter Benjamin West befriended Sully; according to Dunlap, West was like a father to him, and offered the young art-

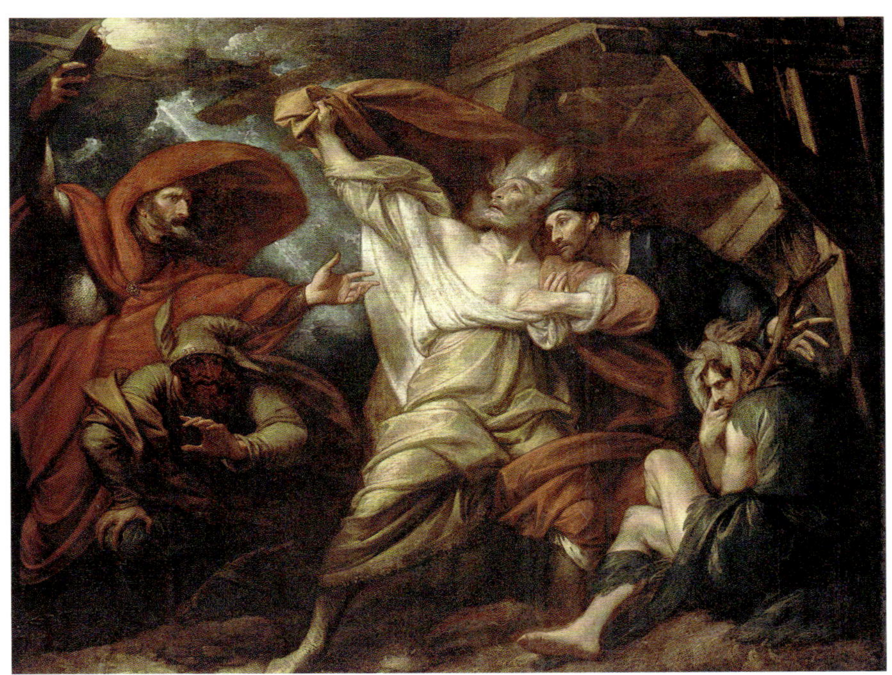

Benjamin West,
King Lear,
1788–1806

ist "the advantage of his instruction and the free use of his pictures."[21] West's grand *King Lear*, painted for Boydell's Shakespeare Gallery, was later purchased by the American inventor and painter Robert Fulton and initially displayed at the Pennsylvania Academy of the Fine Arts in Sully's eventual hometown of Philadelphia.[22] As an avid student of art history with a theatrical bent, Sully may have been inspired in part by Boydell's efforts to prove that there was a worthy school of historical painting in England. West's Shakespearean scene, with its emotionally charged compression of the subjects and dynamic sweep of their gestures across the composition, directed from the central, dominating figure of King Lear to both sides of the canvas, may have further stoked Sully's imagination and his placement of Washington at center stage, with the events

Anthony van Dyck, *Charles the First with M. San Antoine*, 1633

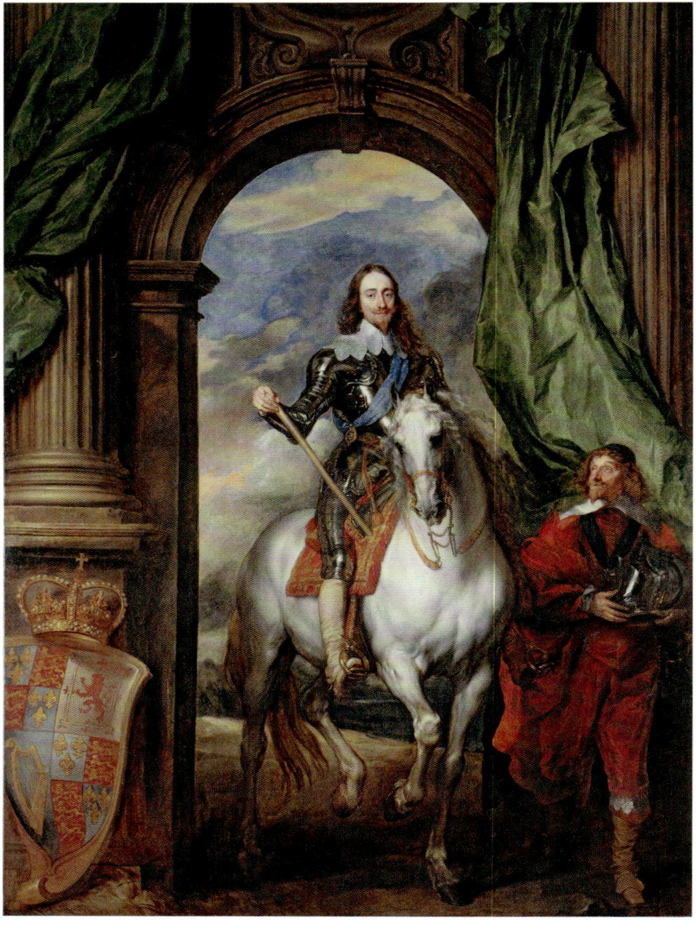

of the nighttime crossing unfolding forcefully to the left and right.

Further contributing to the theatricality of Sully's composition is his masterful handling of natural and stage lighting. The tail of Washington's horse blowing in the stiff gale balances the strands of roots exposed on the riverbank, linking the foreground and the background and framing for our attention the ruddy sunrise breaking through an icy mist. Washington intended his unit to cross the Delaware by midnight, although it was after three o'clock before the last man reached the shore of New Jersey.[23] And yet, to signal the brilliant future for the Continental Army and the cause of liberty, Sully invokes artistic license by depicting a new dawn for the patriot cause. Washington and his steed appear bathed in a light from a source that emanates from outside the scene, to the left of the composition and roughly where viewers stand to face the central protagonist. Sully's light source conjures up the realm of theatrical spectacle rather than nature observed: the otherworldly appearance of Washington recalls the glow of actors' faces lit by footlights at the edge of a stage.

In forging a style of historical portraiture appropriate for the founding father of the United States, Sully turned to models from European history painting that portrayed royal heads of state on horseback. While in London, he would have had an opportunity to study firsthand several great equestrian portraits from the brush of the seventeenth-century Flemish master Peter Paul Rubens, along with those of his student, Anthony van Dyck.[24] Van Dyck's *Charles the First with M. San Antoine* may have intrigued Sully as a source for *The Passage of the Delaware*: the composition presents the king of England riding a white steed in the company of the Master of the Art of Horsemanship, San Antoine. In Sully's composition, the figure on foot who gazes up at the general and holds out his stirrup in preparation to mount, and who bears a sword and wears a blanket coat over his uniform in the extreme cold, may be an officer.

Although Sully had hoped to visit France, he was dissuaded by Benjamin West, who urged the younger artist to stay in London and "improve yourself by copying some pictures." He added, "My collection, old and new, is at your service. There are specimens of the ancient masters and of the moderns. Take them as you want them,

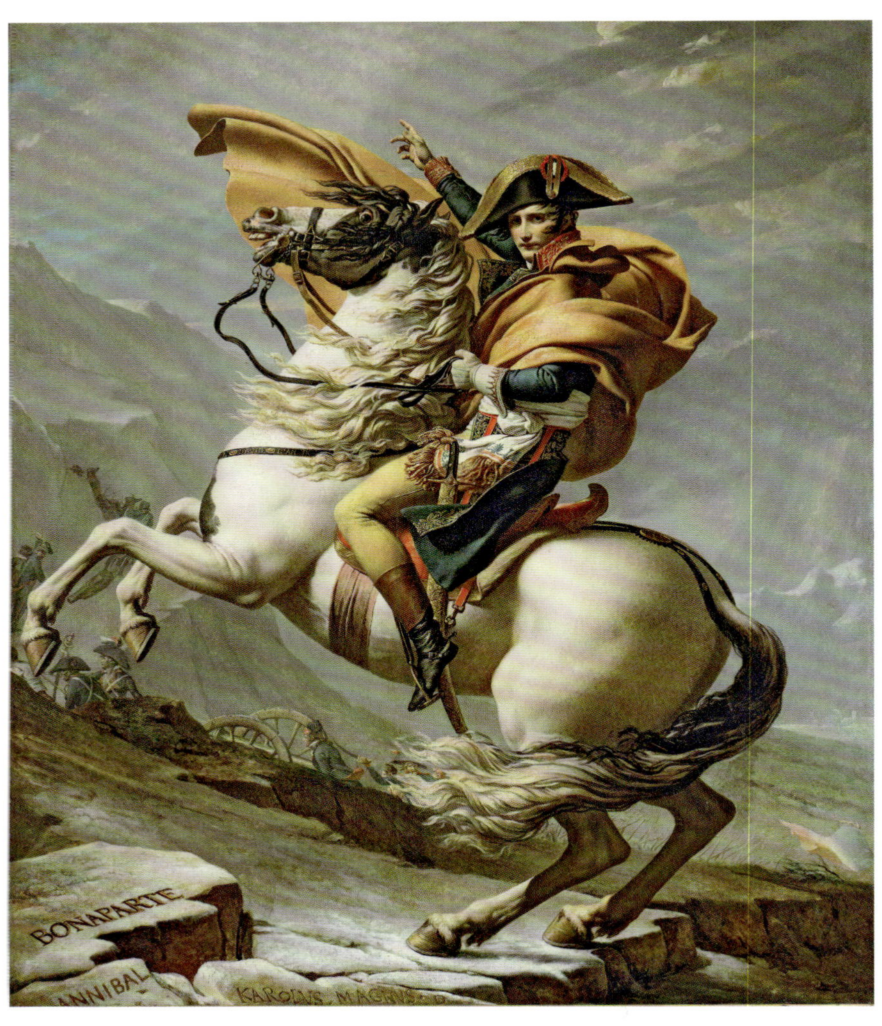

Jacques-Louis David, *Napoleon Crossing the Alps*, 1801

and come to me for my advice when you want it."[25] Even if Sully never crossed the Channel, he would surely have known the compositions of one of the foremost painters of French history, Jacques-Louis David, and his student, Baron Antoine-Jean Gros, whose works were exhibited at the Louvre in Paris and were widely available in engraved reproductions.[26] David painted his iconic equestrian portrait *Napoleon Crossing the Alps* in five versions, initially at the request of the French Ambassador as a diplomatic gift to the King of Spain. In it he situates Napoleon's crossing in the historical record of antiquity, prominently featuring the inscription of Hannibal's name in the left foreground, as a reminder to viewers that the Roman army had been led through the treacherous mountain passes by a consul who traditionally rode a white stallion.

Sully's own compilation "Hints for Pictures" frequently mentions West, also from Pennsylvania, who rose to prominence in London to become the second president of the Royal Academy, in 1792.[27] West's *Death of General Wolfe* was a watershed in painting contemporary history. The clusters of figures flanking the dying General Wolfe, their heads close together as they manifest a range of emotions through facial expressions and gestures, share an affinity with Sully's own compact arrangement of officers and aides on the right-hand side of *The Passage of the Delaware.*

As Sully developed his concept of the historical portrait for an American audience, he may have turned to the work of another important American expatriate painter living in London, John Singleton Copley, who had also made significant contributions to the genre of history painting. The size and drama of Copley's *Death of Major Peirson*, measuring some eight by twelve feet, could have played into Sully's composition. Peirson's death unfolds at the center of a maelstrom of soldiers and civilians, fleeing the shallow space of a city square hemmed in by buildings that suggest painted theatrical scenery flats. The action originates at the left, with the figure of a wounded solder gesturing with his outstretched arm to Major Peirson, who falls to the ground, bleeding from a bullet to the chest. At the right, a woman clutches her child to her breast as she rushes to escape the pandemonium. The theatricality of Sully's *Passage of the*

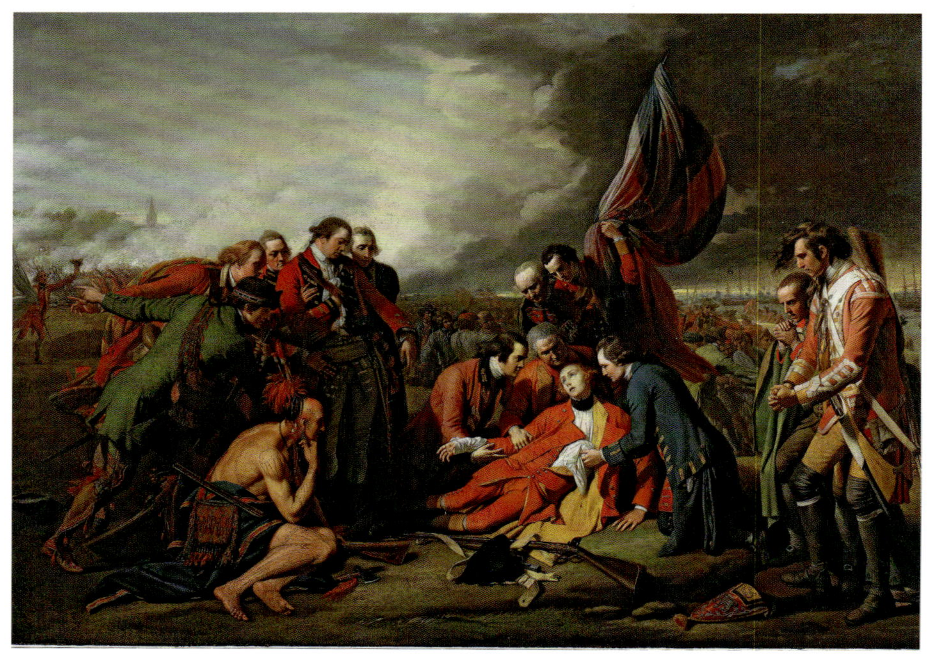

Benjamin West, *The Death of General Wolfe*, 1771

Delaware echoes the scale and dynamic thrust of Copley's painting, even as it evokes the stoic restraint Washington demonstrated on the eve of battle.

To produce a historical portrait worthy of the North Carolina commission, Sully needed to ensure that it would resonate with the formidable array of images of George Washington that were already known to the American public, as well as meet viewers' keen observation of historical details. The accuracy of Washington's portrait was on Sully's mind from the outset; in a letter to Daniel L. Peck, the lawyer charged with executing the artist's contract, Sully noted: "We have in the Pennsylvania Academy of Fine Arts a full length portrait of Genl Washington painted by Stuart for Mr. Bingham, which I can borrow for the purpose of making a copy. . . . We have also in the Academy

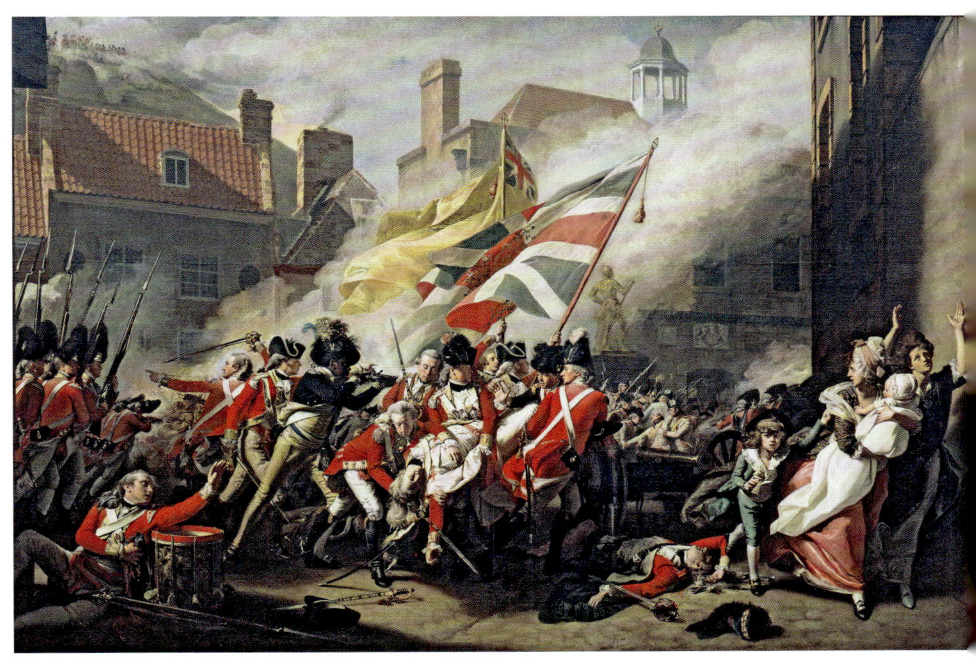

John Singleton Copley, *The Death of Major Peirson*, 1783

of Fine Arts, an original bust of Washington, sculptured by the famous Carraci." In June 1817 Sully returned to the topic of the marble likeness of Washington, as he was concluding negotiation of the terms of the commission: "Am I at liberty to select the Face of Washington from the most approved likeness extant? I must impress upon your recollection that the circumstances of history which I should paint, would require a younger person by twenty years than Stewart's picture represents. In which case the Busts of Hudon & Carraci would be more proper; particularly as the likeness is thought superior, by many competent judges."

The European sculptors Sully mentions, Jean-Antoine Houdon and Giuseppe Ceracchi, had both modeled Washington from life. Houdon made a plaster life mask that captures his features and expressions in late middle

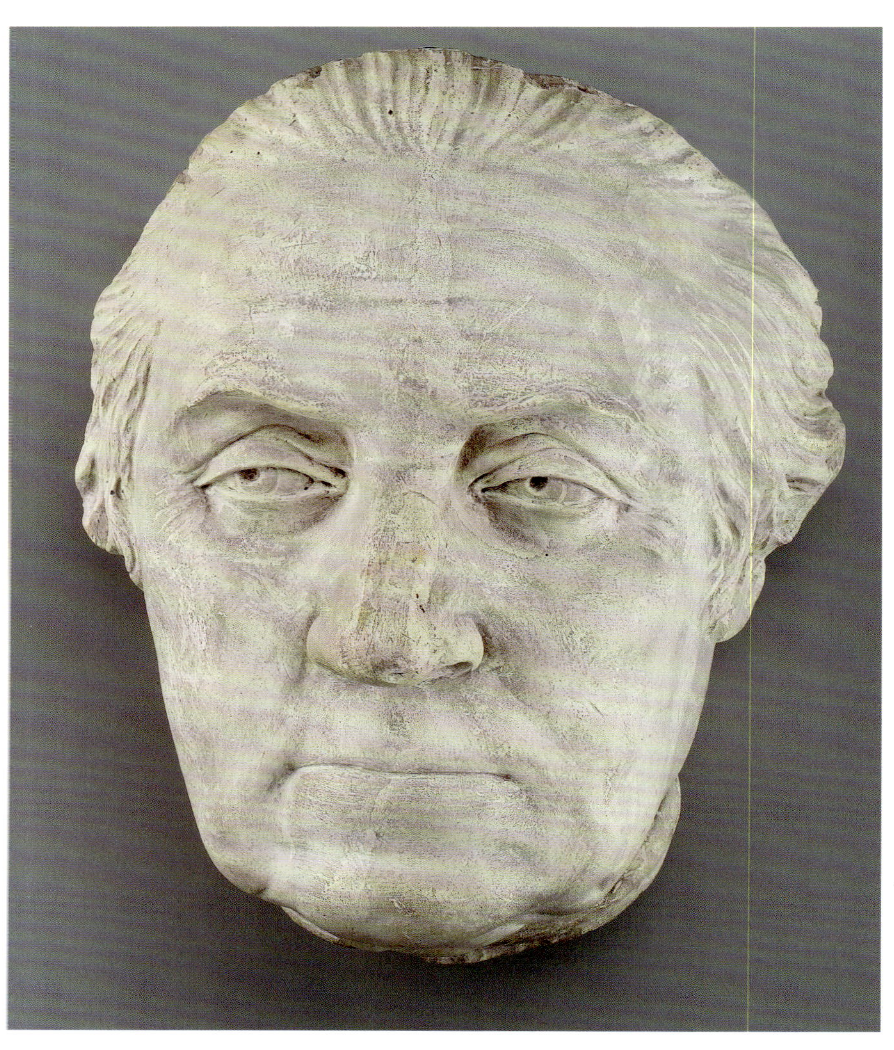

After Jean-Antoine Houdon, *George Washington*, probably early 19th century

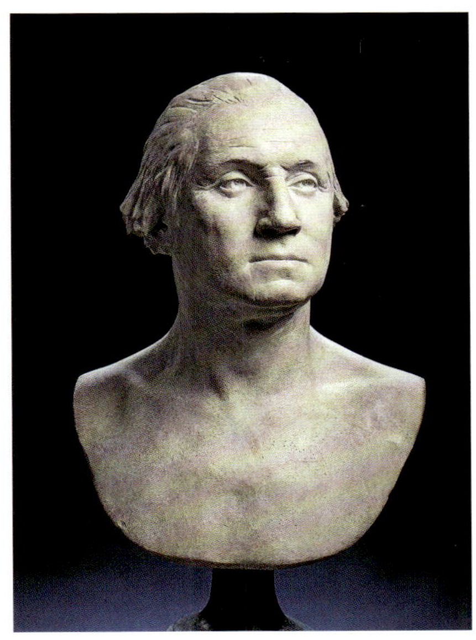

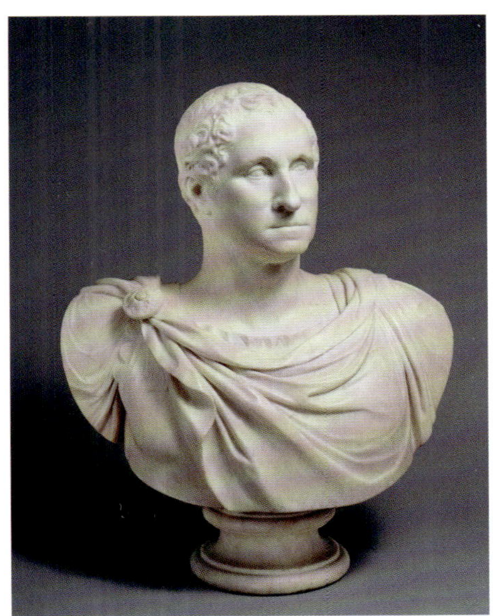

Jean-Antoine Houdon, *Bust of George Washington*, 1785

Giuseppe Ceracchi, *George Washington*, 1795

age, closer to his actual age of 44 at the time he led the Continental Army across the Delaware in 1776. For his rendering in low-fired clay and in marble, Houdon had studied Washington in 1785 at the age of 53, as he went about his daily routine at Mount Vernon. The sculptor eventually settled upon a likeness and expression purportedly inspired by the general's indignant reaction to a high price he was quoted for a horse, modeling Washington's broad brow, firm jawline, and serene countenance, as he gazes into the distance.[28] Houdon gives an impression of Washington's composure and service to a power higher than himself, traits that were highlighted in contemporary biographies such as one by Chief Justice John Marshall, and an interpretation that Sully underscores with his theatrical lighting of Washington's face. If Sully was inspired by Houdon to depict Washington as caught up in his own thoughts, the painter may have looked to the bust by

Ceracci for a sense of Washington's stoicism, determination, and self-sacrifice: he appears as a formidable Roman general, with closely cropped hair and with the folds of his toga draped rigidly over his chest.

Among painted portraits of his subject that Sully would have had direct access to, the earliest and most frequently copied portrayal of the scene was Charles Willson Peale's *George Washington after the Battle of Princeton*, painted from life by the artist, who had served under Washington in the Revolution's battles in New Jersey. Peale portrays the general in a gently curving pose that projects a relaxed, confident manner, signaled by the nonchalant gesture of holding his hat in his hand as he leans against a French cannon. These portable and potent brass field guns, identified by their decorative arching dolphin handles, were part of the artillery clandestinely sent by France in support of the Revolutionary cause that ultimately tipped the scale in favor of the Continental Army.[29] Washington's features are alight with a knowing half-smile that may further be a sly allusion to his savvy use of espionage throughout the Revolution, and especially to gain the advantage at the battles of Trenton and Princeton.

In Sully's painting, the mounted figure of Washington appears adjacent to the cannon heading down the riverbank, with the flourishes of the fins and ridges on the curved dolphin handles clearly depicted. Like Peale, Sully emphasizes the ease and elegance of Washington's posture, here as the graceful and fearless equestrian he was known to be, frequently commented on by his contemporaries, including Thomas Jefferson.[30] Preparing to cross the Delaware, the general appears in striking equipoise between knightly warfare conducted on horseback and modern combat weapons used for field artillery.

The surrounding landscape within Peale's vertical format stretches toward the horizon at the left, a feature that

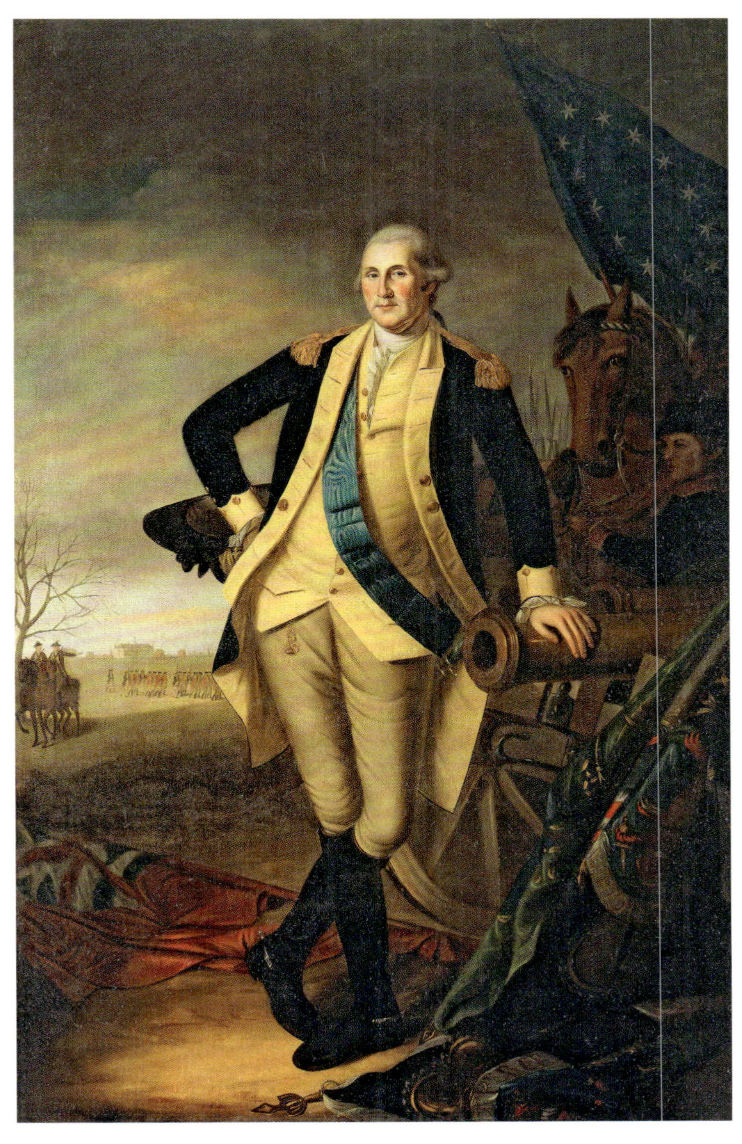

Charles Willson Peale, *George Washington after the Battle of Princeton*, 1779–82

Sully expands greatly in his own sweeping panoramic composition. Although the actual crossing of the Delaware was from west to east, the opening of the vista to the west at the left of the canvas is consistent with conventional orientations of maps depicting North America. Emanuel Leutze, in his later monumental images of the dramatic crossing, maintained the same direction of the action (see p. 48), but in a manner that sets the stage for more explicit visual depictions of manifest destiny in Leutze's later scenes, such as *Westward the Course of Empire Takes Its Way* (1872, United States Capitol).[31]

Besides Charles Willson Peale, the patriot-painter best known by and closest to Sully was John Trumbull. While Sully was living in Charleston, South Carolina, between 1793 and 1794, he was able to study firsthand one of Trumbull's portraits of Washington poised for battle. As many American artists had before him, Sully in 1806 commissioned a portrait from Trumbull, of his wife, so that he "might see his mode of painting, and have a specimen from his pencil."[32] When Sully moved to Hartford, Connecticut, the following year, he worked briefly as a studio assistant to Trumbull. Later, in New York City, Sully may have sought out Trumbull's scenes of the American Revolution, on view at the American Academy by October 1816.[33] At least two of Trumbull's paintings of Washington may have influenced Sully's own historical portrait, and his other battles scenes may have inspired details of costume, features that were of keen interest to both artists. The first was *Washington at Verplanck's Point* (1790, Winterthur Museum), said to be Martha Washington's favorite rendition of her husband, one for which Trumbull noted: "every part of the Dress, the Horse & horse furniture were carefully painted from real objects:—the background represents the encampment of the American Army at Verplanck's point on the North River, Stony Point, & Highlands where the French troops crossed are seen in the distance." Although Martha Washington's small version of the scene remained in her family, Sully would have been able to examine Trumbull's much larger, related *Washington and the Departure of the British Garrison from New York City* (1790), painted for New York's City Hall.[34]

When Trumbull returned to the subject two years later in *General George Washington at Trenton* (1792, Yale University Art Gallery), he juxtaposed the figure of Washington with his steed rearing up in fear behind him, as a young officer struggles to gain control of the horse. Although the artist considered the painting his best work, when it was submitted to the leaders of Charleston, South Carolina, to commemorate Washington's visit there in 1791, city officials refused to accept it; according to the artist, they "would be better satisfied with a more matter-of-fact likeness [of Washington], such as they had recently seen—calm, tranquil, peaceful."[35] Returning to his easel, Trumbull altered the general's pose and turned the horse's hindquarters to expose its raised tail, perhaps signaling a scatological surprise for the city of Charleston, clearly visible on the distant horizon and framed between the horse's hind legs. Trumbull's painting was displayed in Charleston, where Sully could have studied it during his early training there.[36]

Sully also studied with another notable portrayer of Washington, the Boston-based painter Gilbert Stuart. While in Boston, Sully would have been able to see Stuart's grand, full-length portrait *Washington at Dorchester Heights*, commissioned for the Independence Day celebrations of July 4, 1806.[37] This composition also prominently features the hindquarters of Washington's horse, emphasizing the dynamic sweep of the horse's tail. The bulging rear flanks, the seat of the animal's physical strength, could be taken as a symbol of the brazen show of force by the Continental Army's artillery assembled on Dorchester Heights. The

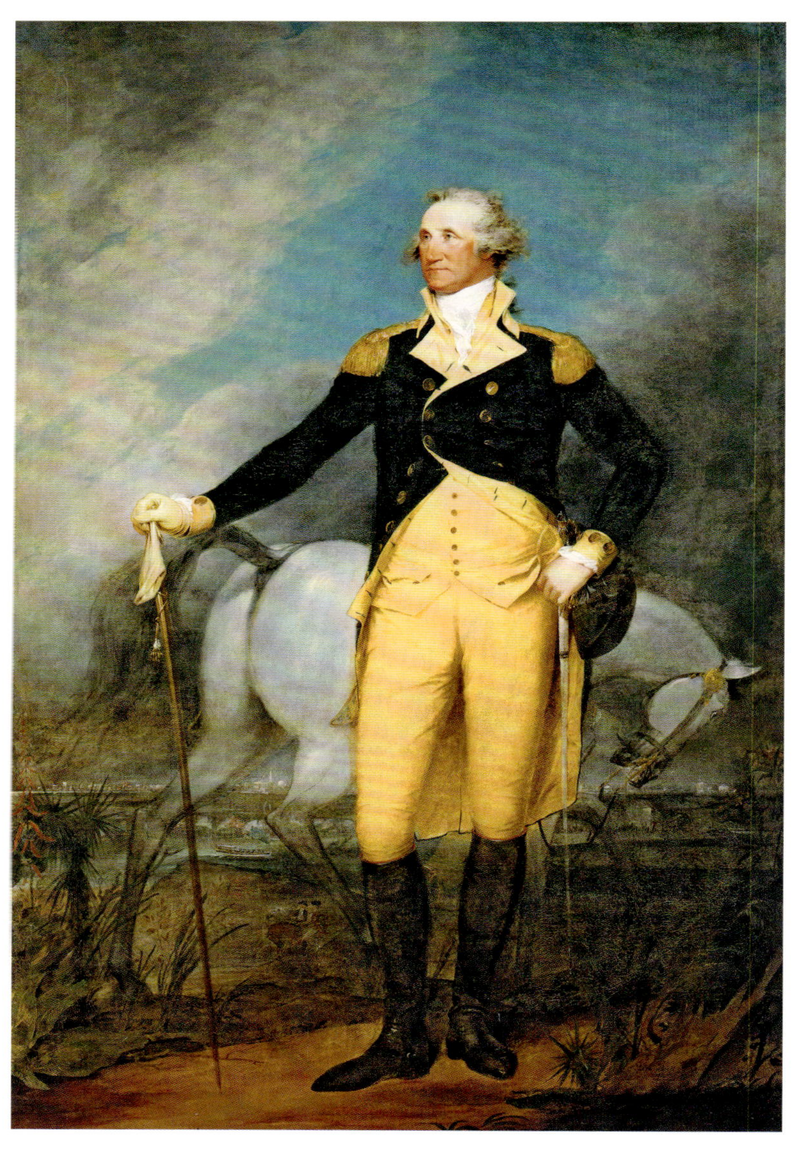

John Trumbull, *Washington at the City of Charleston*, 1792

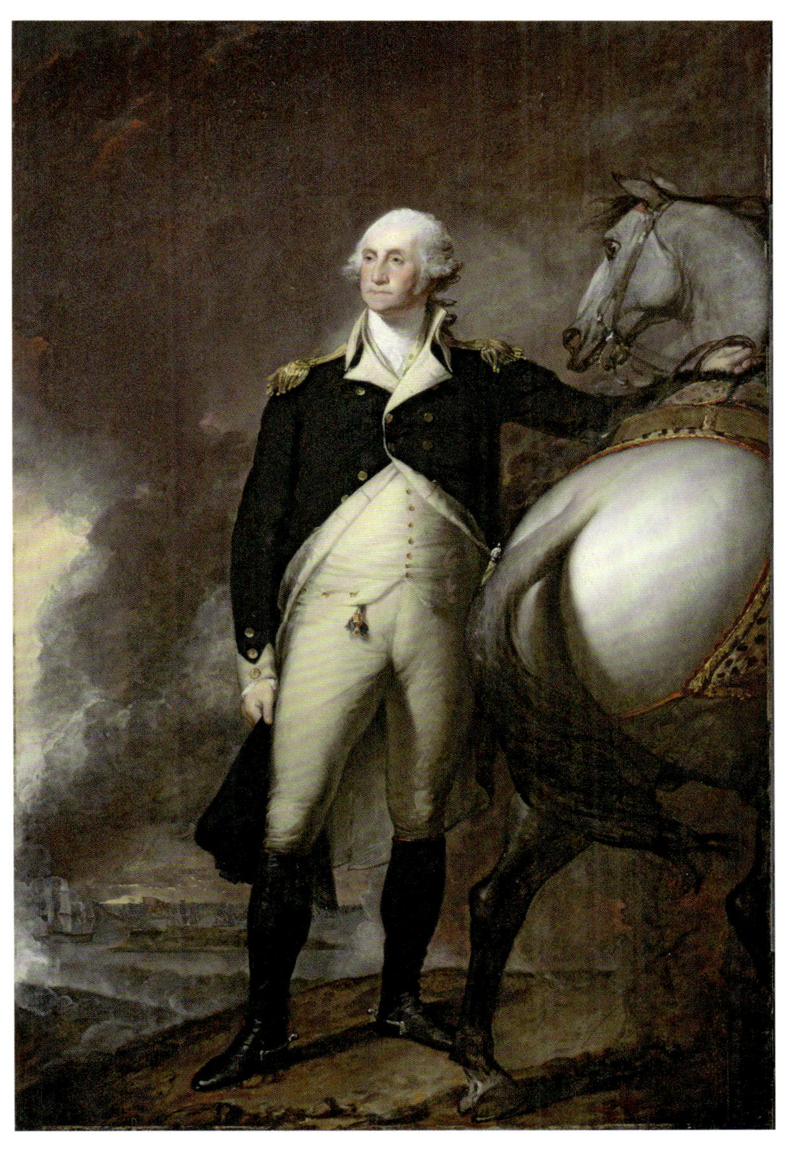

Gilbert Stuart, *Washington at Dorchester Heights*, 1806

British retreat from Boston Harbor, a decisive "turning tail," emboldened the soldiers under Washington's command to persevere.

Sully extended the symbolism of equine subjects in his composition to include a second horse in the group surrounding Washington; this one, seen from behind, a bay with black mane and tail and distinctive white markings on his head and feet, resembles Nelson, the general's favorite mount during battle, known for remaining steady under the siege of artillery. In Sully's painting the bay horse rears its head, a foil to the balletic stance of Washington's white horse and most famous mount during the Revolution, named Blueskin for his blue-gray coloring. In keeping with military traditions dating back to the ancient Romans, Washington rode a white horse in formal processions, often switching from his preferred warhorse, Nelson.[38]

In addition to visual representations of Washington, Sully likely drew on written accounts of the events. The publication of literary tributes to Washington gained momentum after his death in 1799. Among the most popular were moral tales recounted by Mason Locke Weems in his *Life of Washington*, published initially in 1800 with numerous subsequent editions, and perhaps best known for the story of the young Washington refusing to lie about chopping down his father's cherry tree. In his account of the Delaware crossing, Weems highlights Washington's fortitude: Washington and his troops "pressed on through the darksome night, pelted by an incessant storm of hail and snow. . . . But the object before them was too vast to allow one thought about difficulties."[39]

The foremost historical biography, originally issued in 1804 and again in 1807, was Chief Justice Marshall's tome, *The Life of George Washington*. In describing Washington's courage during the winter of 1776, Marshall writes: "Among the many valuable traits in the character of Washington, was that of unyielding firmness which supported him under these accumulated circumstances of depression. Undismayed by the dangers which surrounded him, he did not for an instant relax his exertions, nor omit any thing which could retard the progress of the enemy. He did not appear to despair; and constantly showed himself to his harassed and enfeebled army, with a serene and unembarrassed countenance, betraying no fears in himself, and inspiring others with confidence."[40] Marshall's account and those of eyewitnesses also described Washington fearlessly encouraging the troops on the long route to Trenton, riding up and down the ranks, exhorting them to "March on! My brave fellows! After me!"[41] By evoking the accounts of Marshall and Weems, Sully's painting reveals an agile balance of historical fact with popular, apocryphal tales surrounding the life of Washington to render a theatrical form of historical fiction and a memorable historical portrait.

Although Sully was an accomplished portraitist and carefully documented the production of his works, only three figures in *The Passage of the Delaware* can be identified with certainty. First and foremost, of course, is George Washington himself: poised with his hand on his hip, looking away from us toward the river he is about to cross, he is every inch the Commander-in-Chief. Washington's interest in cultivating correct bearing, comportment, and manners began in his teens, when he hand-copied a publication titled *Rules of Civility*.[42] As a military leader, he was a stickler for proper uniforms, and specified for officers in the Continental Army a blue jacket with buff-colored facings, adorned with simple, flat brass buttons, based on uniforms for the militia he commanded in 1774.[43] He would maintain this color scheme throughout his life, as seen in his only surviving uniform (1789, National Museum of American History). In the field, Washington preferred to

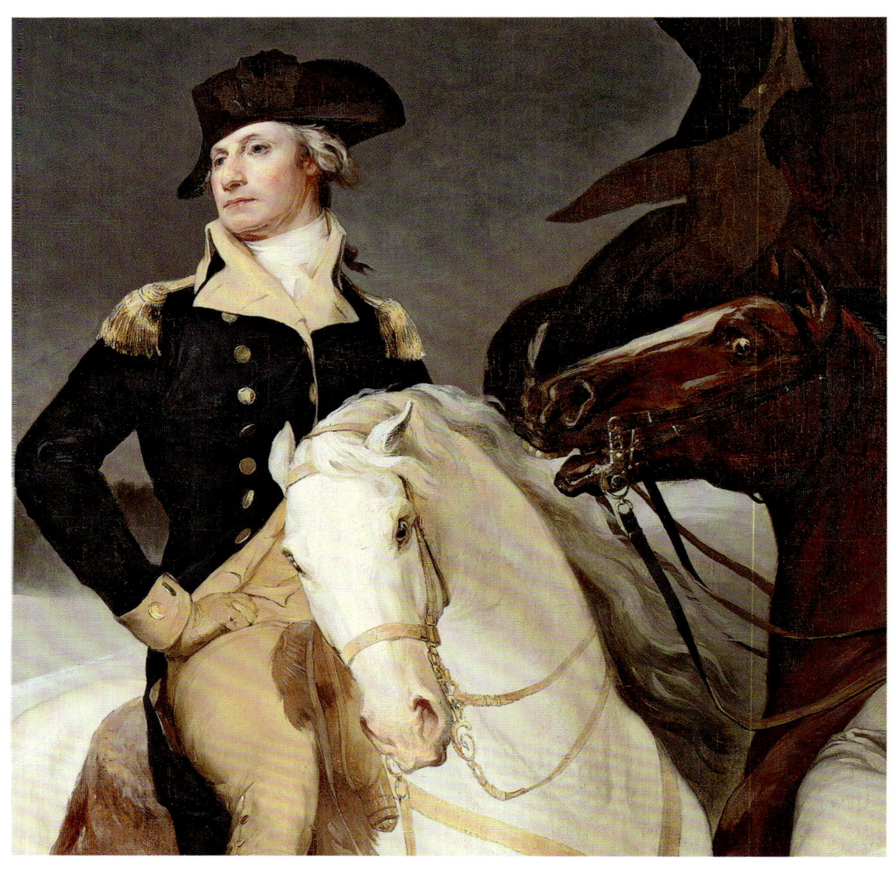

wear more practical and durable buckskin breeches; for his dress uniform, he had an eye for a bit of flash, specifying epaulettes of gold lace and bullion fringe, details that Sully obliging rendered. The general also adopted the tricorn hat, with black ribbon cockade worn by officers. This distinction was not lost on Sully, who placed both his signature and the *TS* monogram he attached to "fancy pictures" on Washington's hat, details that recently came to light during conservation treatments on the painting.[44] Another signature on the black band of the aide-de-camp's blanket coat also emerged during cleaning, presumably located where it could be seen more easily by viewers standing in front of the enormous composition. Sully further documented his presence in the scene by including his reflection as seen from behind as he bends over an enormous canvas, leaning on a mahlstick, in one of the flat surfaces of Washington's buttons, along with the horse's head and ear.

The officer rising behind Washington on a rearing horse and brandishing a sword is General Henry Knox. Born in Boston, Knox witnessed the Boston Massacre in 1770, later testifying at the trials of the British soldiers. During the winter of 1775, he famously led the transport of cannons from Fort Ticonderoga, on Lake Champlain, some three hundred miles overland to Dorchester Heights, thereby hastening the British withdrawal of occupation from Boston and scoring a decisive victory for the American cause. As Washington prepared to cross the Delaware River on Christmas night of 1776, Knox was again in charge of the artillery forces; his commanding presence at the uppermost of the group of officers gives visual expression to the sound of his voice carrying above the fray. Sully further emphasizes Knox's resolve in the face of severe winter conditions by showing misty breath rising from the nostrils and muzzle of his horse into the freezing cold night air.

Other officers attending to Washington that night cannot be identified with certainty, although the most likely candidate for the man at the far right is General Nathaniel Greene, who was given the most difficult overland route to Trenton following the treacherous crossing.[45] Sully may have selected this figure to honor the commissioners of the historical portrait: later in the war, Greene served as Commander of the Continental Army throughout the southern states, a post he formally accepted on December 2, 1780, in Charlotte, North Carolina. Some years earlier, Sully had been commissioned to portray another event in

Greene's career, when he presided over the trial of Major André (1812, Worcester Art Museum). The figure's distinctive bushy eyebrows and aquiline nose suggest that this is a portrait of a particular officer in Washington's circle. The apparent age of the man matches that of General Greene in 1776, and he resembles the miniature of Greene that Sully's mentor Trumbull painted from life (1792, Yale University Art Gallery).[46]

The figure bending down below Greene, with a sliver of his face peeking out beneath his officer's cap and the turned-up collar of his blanket coat, remains unidentified. Bearing a sword and the youthful appearance of Washington's aides-de-camp, this man may represent a combination of several different officers. Following the Battle of Trenton, on New Year's Eve 1776, Thomas Mifflin, a socially prominent former aide-de-camp from Philadelphia noted for his participation in the battles of New Jersey, appeared "mounted on a noble looking horse and clothed in an overcoat made up of a large rose blanket and a large fur cap on his head," as he implored the troops who had completed the term of their enlistment to fight on in the Battle of Princeton.[47]

A second candidate is Samuel B. Webb, another important aide-de-camp from Washington's circle, who attended him at the Delaware crossing, and was an officer known for his facility with horses as well as his ability to draft dispatches neatly and precisely in the field. Charles Willson Peale considered his miniature portrait of Webb, which exists in at least three versions (Webb-Deane-Stevens House; New-York Historical Society; and private collection), to be one of his best likenesses. Webb's prominent nose and dark features as painted by Peale are consistent with the few facial details Sully provides. Sully's placement of Webb looking up at Washington may also be connected with the artist's awareness of the extensive journals

John Trumbull,
Self-Portrait, 1777

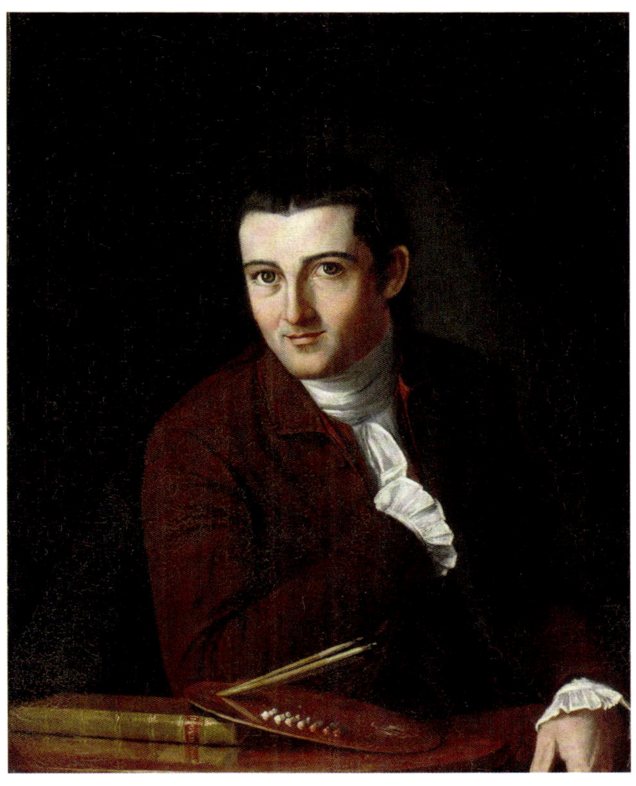

the aide kept during his eight years in the Continental Army. Sully could have known about the archive through John Trumbull, who was related to Webb by marriage and like him belonged to a stalwart circle of patriots from the Connecticut River Valley.[48] Webb may also have embodied the determination and fearlessness of the young officers present at the Delaware crossing: he was given the job of relaying Washington's explicit orders to "use the bayonet and penetrate into the town" of Trenton should damp powder in the troops' muskets fail to fire.[49]

Another candidate is Sully's teacher John Trumbull, who cannot be placed definitively at the scene, although he was serving in the Continental Army and was said to be in Newtown soon after the battle of Trenton. He was surely the foremost portraitist informing *The Passage of the Delaware* by his dynamic sketches and paintings of the event. By choosing to paint a monumental scene of Washington preparing for the Battle of Trenton, Sully followed closely in his teacher's footsteps. Trumbull stated his aspirations as a history painter in a letter to his father from London in 1784: "The great object of my wishes . . . is to take up the History of Our Country, and paint the principal Events particularly of the last War: but this is a work which to execute with any degree of honour or profit, will require very great powers & those powers must be attained before I leave Europe."[50] Trumbull resigned from the Continental Army in 1777 to devote himself to painting, with a particular focus on the American Revolution. That same year, he painted a self-portrait, depicting a forehead and prominent nose, as well as a dark complexion, similar to those of the officer in the foreground of Sully's composition. It would be fitting for Sully to hide a portrait of Trumbull in plain sight, placed directly below General Washington, as the artist closest to both the Commander-in-Chief and Sully himself. Or Sully may have envisioned the officer as an imaginary combination of Webb, a consummate historian of the Revolution, and Trumbull, the consummate Revolutionary portraitist.

Central to the cluster of three men is another figure on horseback whose identity is sure, but whose role in the composition is complex. The man to the left of General Greene is an enslaved African American, William (Billy) Lee, who was at Washington's side throughout the Revolution. Lee performed the duties of a valet by attending to Washington's attire and grooming, among other needs, returning to their home at Mount Vernon only twice during eight years of waging war. Washington had purchased William Lee in 1768 for 61 pounds and 15 shillings—the

John Trumbull, *George Washington*, 1780

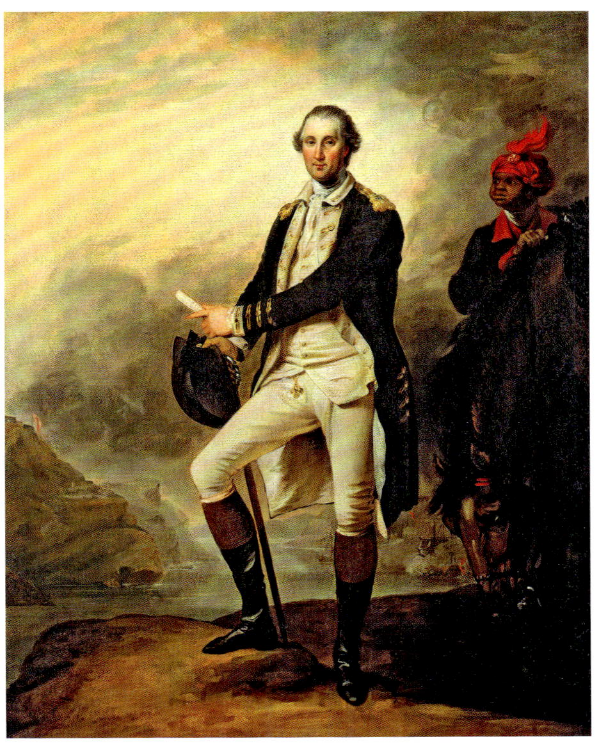

rough equivalent of the price of four horses—and also acquired his younger brother, Frank Lee, both described as mulattos, from Mary Smith Ball Lee, the widow of Colonel John Lee, who was the eldest son of Henry Lee.[51] Sully portrays Lee dressed in a peaked fur hat like those in Trumbull's scene of General Montgomery and American officers fighting the British at the Battle of Quebec of December 31, 1775.[52] The headgear worn by civilians and officers in extreme cold represents a distinct departure from the more traditional knotted kerchief that Lee dons in Trumbull's portrait of George Washington. Sully paints Lee in a brown coat with a leather cross-strap and accompanying shoulder belt plate, details from military dress that highlight his responsibility for Washington's "most precious" papers and his spyglass.[53] The spyglass was one of the general's most important possessions, dating from his early years as a surveyor, and an instrument that in warfare could determine "Victory or Death" by detecting enemy movements and revealing elements of the terrain.

Whereas earlier portraits positioned Lee subservient to Washington, in Sully's painting he is mounted on horseback and elevated above the two soldiers in the foreground, effectively placed on equal footing with the horsemen surrounding him: Washington, Knox, and Greene. Like Washington, Lee was a legendary rider: a description of his wildly unconventional manner when following the hounds in Virginia records that "throwing himself almost at length on the animal, with his spur in flank, this fearless horseman would rush, at full speed, through brake or tangled wood, in a style at which modern huntsmen would stand aghast."[54]

To begin to understand the implications of Lee's portrait within *The Passage of the Delaware*, it is important to consider Washington's own position on slavery as it evolved over time, along with that of the nation, in the context of a passionately contested, transatlantic debate. Washington owned slaves from the time he was a young boy until his death. He began purchasing slaves before his 1759 marriage to Martha Custis, the richest widow in Virginia, which brought an additional eighty-four "dower slaves" to his property, and continued to acquire slaves until the late 1780s. Yet by 1775 Washington was leading a racially integrated army, following his proposal to enlist free blacks; and by 1778 he maintained, "I every day long more and more to get clear" of the institution of slavery.[55]

Within the composition, William Lee's head may be seen as a visual pendant to George Washington's. Whereas the general's face is brightly lit as he turns to his right to survey the Pennsylvania landscape, Lee, at the same level as Washington, is in shadow and turns his darker features in the opposite direction. Situated between the Commander-in-Chief and one of the leading generals that night, Lee looks directly, yet slightly upward, at Greene. The artist calls attention to the encounter of these two men by juxtaposing their features and headgear; Greene's distinctive profile, with his cocked hat sporting a large plume, creates a striking counterpart to Lee's peaked fur cap. Sully was aware that his painting was meant to hang in a state that tolerated slavery, yet, as a Unitarian working in Philadelphia, a city that staunchly supported abolition, he bestows greater prominence on the role of Lee in Washington's army than Peale or Trumbull did in their earlier portraits, depicting him as a central participant in the midst of the historic events.

By the end of Washington's life, several factors had convinced him to free Lee, along with all his other slaves: he was well aware of the moral arguments that slavery was evil, as was repeatedly emphasized by many distinguished members of his circle whom he respected. He also had amassed enough of a fortune to be able to afford to free his slaves. Finally, he knew that prominent members of the international community decried the United States' failure to provide the inalienable rights of freedom, so hard won during the American Revolution, to enslaved people. One of the most intriguing insights into Washington's attitudes towards abolition is found in a book from his library, a leather volume embossed with the title "Tracts on Slavery" that binds together a series of contemporary antislavery pamphlets and bears his signature.[56] On the afternoon of his death, Washington instructed his wife, Martha, to retrieve one of two wills and burn the other; the document that ultimately governed his estate effectively freed all 124

and painting one of a scale proportion'd to the place you have described in your letter: say 9 x 7 feet." Eventually the artist and the North Carolina legislature agreed to dispense with another portrait of Washington, and Sully ultimately retained his painting, declaring: "I cheerfully withdraw any claim I may be thought to have had: at the same time professing myself happy to receive from that honorable body any order they may at a future time think proper to distinguish me with."[62]

Over time, the artist seems to have developed a distaste for the painting; Dunlap reports that when Sully later heard the picture mentioned, he sometimes said, "I wish it were burnt." Though the source of Sully's disregard for the painting is unclear, Dunlap assesses that the young artist would have expended some "thousands of dollars" to produce it and notes as well the challenges for any artist successfully to paint history instead of portraits. The biographer judges *The Passage of the Delaware* both a great success and an unmitigated failure: "Mr. Sully had produced a fine historical picture, representing perhaps the most brilliant achievement of Washington, and in many respects in the most perfect style of art. [Unfortunately] Washington's portrait was not acknowledged as a likeness. . . . If it was an old instead of a modern picture, the winter landscape would alone stamp it as a jewel; but in the old pictures one good part redeems—in the modern, one part faulty condemns."[63]

Free of the North Carolina commission, *The Passage of the Delaware* embarked on a national tour, appearing as far south as Norfolk, Virginia, in a space scouted by Dunlap.[64] The composition also was exhibited in Philadelphia, but did not attract a buyer until it reached Boston, where it was purchased by the frame maker and picture dealer John Doggett for $500. He exhibited it in his Repository of Arts, located on Market Street, between April and June 1823, but ultimately sold it at auction to Ethan A. Greenwood, who displayed the painting in Portland, Maine.[65] By 1841 the painting had changed hands and was owned by the Boston Museum and Gallery of Fine Arts, established by Moses Kimball in a building that flanked the Boston Common on Tremont and Bromfield Streets. A wood engraving of the interior shows *The Passage of the Delaware* hanging prominently on the back wall amid a miscellany of works of art, classical statuary, and natural history specimens, including an elegant giraffe. When the Boston Museum relocated to the corner of Tremont and School Streets in November 1846, the *Boston Daily Transcript* highlighted the installation of the painting over the staircase.[66]

By this time, the cult of Washington had gathered full steam. The public display of Sully's painting itself inspired artists of all abilities, including the self-taught Edward Hicks, who painted his own version of the scene that was displayed at the Pennsylvania site of the historic crossing. When the revolutions of 1848 swept Europe, the German-American artist Emanuel Leutze set out to create his own monumental conception of *Washington Crossing the Delaware*, which replaced Sully's composition as the most frequently reproduced version of the scene, in a range of popular prints. The Currier and Ives firm, founded in 1857, made the image of *Washington Crossing the Delaware* nearly ubiquitous through its widely distributed hand-colored lithographs.[67] During the Civil War, Abraham Lincoln endowed Washington's crossing with new meaning, declaring in 1861: "Of [Washington's] struggles none fixed itself on my mind so indelibly as the crossing of the Delaware preceding the Battle of Trenton. I remember these great struggles were made for some object. I am exceeding anxious that the object they fought for—liberty, and the Union and the Constitution they formed—shall be perpetual."[68] In a less exalted tone, in 1883 Mark Twain noted in *Life on*

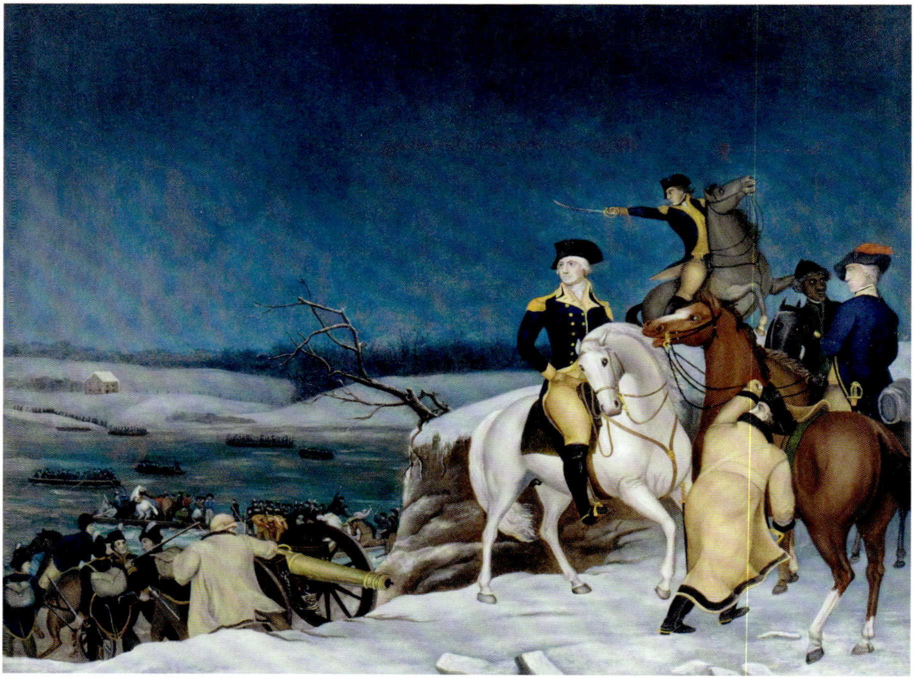

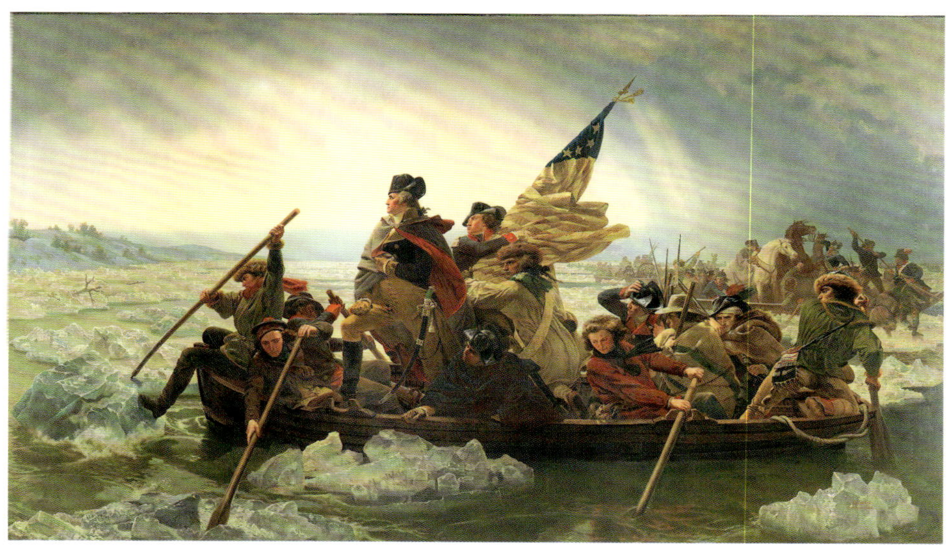

Edward Hicks, *Passage of the Delaware after Sully*, about 1840

Emanuel Leutze, *Washington Crossing the Delaware*, 1851

the Mississippi that within "the residence of the principal citizen, all the way from the suburbs of New Orleans to the edge of St. Louis . . . Over the middle of the mantle, engraving—Washington Crossing the Delaware; on the wall by the door, copy of it done in thunder-and-lightning crewel by the young ladies—work of art which would have made Washington hesitate about the crossing, if he could have foreseen what advantage to be taken of it."[69]

George Washington continued to be held in special esteem in Massachusetts, where the Revolution began and where the general first assumed command of the Continental Army. At the Boston Athenaeum, the original home of Gilbert Stuart's iconic portraits of George Washington and Martha Washington (1796; now Museum of Fine Arts, Boston, and National Portrait Gallery, Washington, D.C.), there are more volumes from Washington's library than are housed at his home at Mount Vernon. The Cambridge-born philanthropist Alice Wadsworth Longfellow, daughter of Henry Wadsworth Longfellow and Fanny Appleton Longfellow, was the longest-serving member of the Mount Vernon Ladies' Association, and in the first decades of its founding, the Museum of Fine Arts purchased a cast of Houdon's life mask (see p. 26).

These preservation efforts joined a great wave of resurgent interest in Washington that continued from midcentury through the Civil War, the nation's centennial, and into the Colonial Revival of the early twentieth century. Many states named prominent parks, public monuments, and universities after Washington, and his face frequently appeared on coins and paper currency. Another important development in keeping the flame of Washington's memory alive was the 1858 purchase of his estate by the Mount Vernon Ladies' Association, which acquired the house and two hundred acres from Washington's great-grandnephew and opened the property to the public in 1860.[70] One of the most impressive late nineteenth-century monuments to Washington was the obelisk on the National Mall of the nation's capital. When it was completed in December 1884, it stood proudly as the tallest building in the world.

In 1903 the Boston Museum was forced to close its doors, and the owners donated *The Passage of the Delaware* to the Museum of Fine Arts, one of the few institutions that could accommodate the painting's massive scale and make it available to a wide public. By the time Sully's historical portrait entered the collection, though, its sweeping view of history was already considered woefully old-fashioned; some ten years earlier a critic had declared: "The only absurdity which mars Sully's art is his 'Washington Crossing the Delaware.' . . . It is one of those historical pieces that remind one of the old traveling panorama."[71] The monumental canvas arrived at the MFA just as the institution was rapidly outgrowing its first home on Copley Square. One of the earliest records of the painting in the new building on Huntington Avenue shows it in the William Morris Hunt Library, in a simple frame. As the museum expanded through the twentieth century, Sully's picture was prominently displayed in several locations. The painting is now on view in the Art of the Americas Wing, the first work of art to be installed before the building opened on November 20, 2010, and for the first time displayed at the MFA in its original frame.[72] Surrounding Sully's masterpiece are works of art in the Neoclassical style that speak to the young nation's ambition to create symbolism worthy of its new government, leaders, and citizens. Today, Sully's *Passage of the Delaware* continues to express the bold ambitions of the Revolutionary patriots as well as the identity of the nation in its early decades, all the while challenging our understanding of how art can shape collective history.

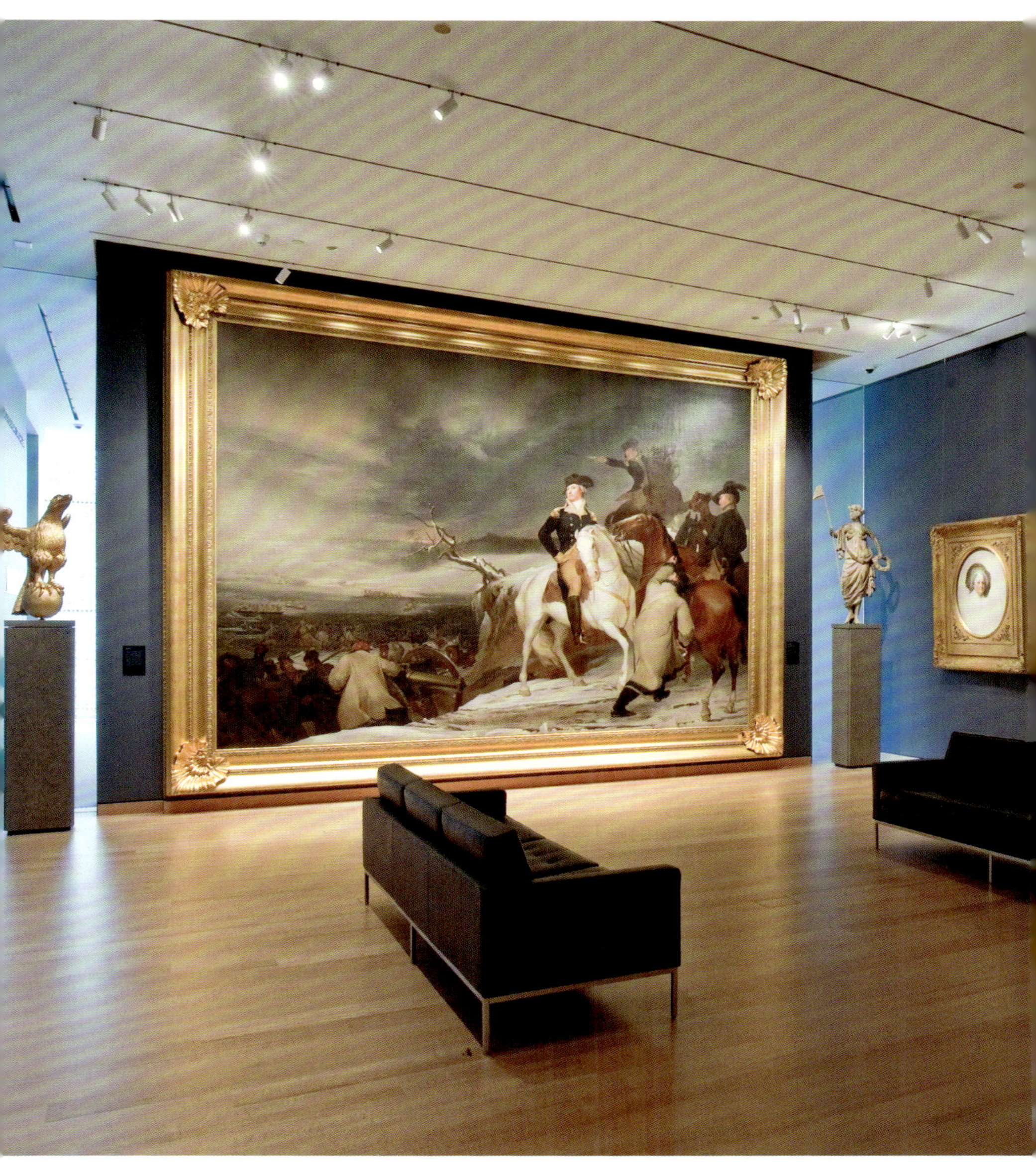

The Passage of the Delaware, in original frame by John Doggett, in the Art of the Americas Wing, Museum of Fine Arts, Boston, 2010

13. See William Keyse Rudolph, "Understanding Sully's Fancy Pictures," pp. 54–85 in Rudolph and Soltis, *Thomas Sully*. See also Carol Troyen, "Thomas Sully's *The Torn Hat*," *Journal of the Museum of Fine Arts, Boston* 4 (1992): 4–16.
14. Dunlap, *History*, 2: 270.
15. Ibid., 2: 272. Quotations here and below from correspondence about the commission are from Fehl, "Thomas Sully's *Washington's Passage*," 596.
16. See Kevin J. Avery, *John Vanderlyn's Panoramic View of the Gardens and Palace of Versailles* (New York: Metropolitan Museum of Art, 1998).
17. See www.worcesterart.org/collection/Early-American/Artists/Penniman/biography (accessed February 17, 2016). See also mention of "a transparent painting, from the Pencil of Penniman, of the Great Fire and Surrounding Scenery," in *The Columbian Centinel* (October 1819), Collections of Historic New England, Boston.
18. Charles Coleman Sellers, *Mr. Peale's Museum: Charles Willson Peale and the First Popular Museum of Natural Science and Art* (New York: Norton, 1980), 13.
19. See Stephen Oettermann, *The Panorama: History of a Mass Medium* (New York: Zone, 1997), 314.
20. Preface to *Boydell's Shakespeare Gallery Portfolio*, London, March 25, 1805; initially published May 1, 1789. Department of Prints, Drawings, and Photographs, MFA, Boston.
21. Dunlap, *History*, 2: 257.
22. Carrie Rebora, "Robert Fulton's Art Collection," *The American Art Journal* 22, no. 3 (1990): 40–63, esp. 47, 57. See also "Benjamin West, *King Lear*, 1788," in *Art of the Americas Paintings Catalogue Online*, www.mfa.org (consulted September 26, 2015).
23. Stryker, *Battles*, 138.
24. For example, Rubens's grand equestrian portrait of the first Duke of Buckingham, which hung at York House in London. A sketch for the portrait (1625) survives at the Kimbell Art Museum, Fort Worth.
25. Dunlap, *History*, 2: 259.
26. Elliot Bostwick Davis, "Currency of Culture: Prints in New York City," in *Art and the Empire City: New York, 1825–1861*, ed. Catherine Hoover Voorsanger and John K. Howat (New York: Metropolitan Museum of Art; New Haven: Yale University Press, 2000), 215.
27. Thomas Sully, "Thomas Sully's Hints for Pictures, 1809–1871; Techniques for Painting Portraits, Ingredients for Colors, Care and Preservation of Paintings, Criticisms for Other Artists, and Explanations of Their Paintings and Techniques," Archives of American Art, Smithsonian Institution, Washington, D.C., roll no. N18, typescript, 179 pp.
28. The story about the horse dealing may be apocryphal; see R. Walton Moore, "General Washington and Houdon," *Virginia Magazine of History and Biography* 41, no. 1 (Jan. 1933): 9.
29. Identification of the artillery known as "four pounders" was made by the military and art historian Christopher Bryant (personal communications, October 2015 and February 2016), who also noted that the negotiations to purchase cannons considered outmoded by the French were conducted discreetly by Samuel B. Webb's stepfather, Silas Deane. These weapons, which became the symbolic cannons of the American cause, were not received until April 1777, but Sully and his viewers would have been unaware of the historical anomaly.
30. Mary V. Thompson, "Horses and

Horsemanship at Mount Vernon," research notes compiled November 16–17, 2009, pp. 12–14.

31. See Thistlethwaite, *Image of George Washington*, 90–91.
32. Dunlap, *History*, 2: 246.
33. Rudolph, "Chronology," 88.
34. John Trumbull to Mrs. E. P. Custis, May 1829. See Edgar P. Richardson, "A Penetrating Characterization of Washington by John Trumbull," *Winterthur Portfolio* 3 (1967): 1–23, esp. 21.
35. Graham C. Boettcher, "The Cult of Washington," entry for John Trumbull, *General George Washington at Trenton* (1792), in Helen Cooper et al., *Life, Liberty, and the Pursuit of Happiness: American Art from the Yale University Art Gallery* (New Haven: Yale University Press), 117. The first painting by Trumbull was retained by him and later donated to the Yale University Art Gallery. The second version, also known as "Trumbull's Revenge," remains in the collection of the City Hall of Charleston.
36. Rudolph, "Chronology," 86.
37. See catalogue entry in *American Paintings in the Museum of Fine Arts, Boston* (Boston: Museum of Fine Arts; Greenwich, CT: New York Graphic Society, 1969), vol. 1, cat. 915, pp. 247–48. See also *Paintings of the Americas*, www.mfa.org/catalogues/paintings-americas.
38. The pose of Washington's horse, with slightly splayed legs, may have been inspired by eyewitness accounts of the general's mount slipping out from under him on the icy riverbank; see Fischer, *Washington's Crossing*, 226–27. See also Thompson, "Horses and Horsemanship at Mount Vernon," 27–39, 106.
39. Mason Locke Weems, *The Life of George Washington; with Curious Anecdotes, Equally Honorable to Himself, and Exemplary to His Young Countrymen* (Philadelphia: Joseph Allen, 1800), 93.
40. John Marshall, *Life of George Washington*, ed. Robert Faulkner and Paul Carrese (Indianapolis: Liberty Fund, 2000), 75.
41. Fischer, *Washington's Crossing*, 243.
42. *George Washington's Rules of Civility and Decent Behaviour in Company and Conversation*, ed. Charles Moore (Boston: Houghton Mifflin, 1926). See also the article on *The Rules of Civility* in *The George Washington Digital Encyclopedia* (accessed February 22, 2016).
43. James L. Kochan, "As Plain as Blue and Buff Could Make It: George Washington's Uniforms as Commander-in-Chief and President, 1775–1799," *The 44th Washington Antiques Show* (1969): 94; posted online at www.jameskochan.com.
44. Ibid., 95; for the use of the *TS* monogram on "fancy pictures," see Rudolph and Soltis, *Thomas Sully: Painted Performance*, 54–85.
45. Fehl, "Thomas Sully's *Washington's Passage*," 591. Fehl, however, notes that the catalogue for the old Boston Museum identifies the two figures as Generals Nathaniel Greene and Daniel Morgan, who was actually serving as a colonel in Virginia in December of 1776, and joined Washington's forces in April of 1777.
46. Fehl observes that "Greene's portraits from life can hardly be reconciled with either one of the faces painted by Sully." Ibid., 591. For a portrait of Greene from life, see Cooper et al., *Life, Liberty, and the Pursuit of Happiness*, cat. 40, p. 98.
47. Fehl, "Thomas Sully's *Washington's Passage*," 592. However, as noted by Christopher Bryant (personal communica-

tion), if Sully were following this eyewitness account, he failed to include the detail of the rose-medallion blanket worn by Mifflin. Mifflin served as Washington's aide-de-camp in 1775, and, according to Samuel B. Webb's papers, was already working as the quartermaster in charge of supplying the troops in December of 1776. See Samuel B. Webb Papers, Yale University, Sterling Library, Box One, Vol. 1, 1764–77.

48. Worthington Chauncey Ford, ed., *Correspondences and Journals of Samuel Blachley Webb* (New York, 1894), 3: 153–54.
49. Stryker, *Battles*, 140. See also James Watson Webb, with Silas Deane and John Austin Stevens, *Reminiscences of Samuel B. Webb of the Revolutionary Army by His Son, J. Watson Webb* (New York, 1882).
50. As quoted in Helen Cooper, *John Trumbull: The Hand and Spirit of a Painter* (New Haven: Yale University Art Gallery, 1982), 5. For Trumbull's own account of the events of December 1776 and the subsequent battles, see *Autobiography, Reminiscences, and Letters of John Trumbull* (New York: Wiley, 1841), 37–38.
51. Mary V. Thompson, "William Lee & Oney Judge: A Look at George Washington and Slavery," *Journal of the American Revolution* (June 19, 2014) http://allthingsliberty.com (accessed March 3, 2015). See also Mary V. Thompson, "Slaves on the Mansion House Farm — 1799," research compilation, p. 31. Colonel and Mrs. Lee had no children; see "Colonel John Lee," in *Lee of Virginia, 1642–1892: Biographical and Genealogical Sketches of the Decendents of Colonel Richard Lee*, ed. Edmund Jennings Lee (Philadelphia, 1895; rept. Baltimore, MD: Genealogical Publishing Company, 1983), 285–87.
52. John Trumbull, *The Death of General Montgomery in the Attack on Quebec, December 31, 1775* (1786, Yale University Art Gallery); Christopher Bryant, personal communication.
53. Thompson, "William Lee & Oney Judge," 5. The association of Washington with his spyglass is borne out by a watercolor by John J. Stone, *George Washington on Horseback Holding Field Glass* (Museum of Fine Arts, Boston, 60.1124).
54. Quoted in Thompson, "Horses and Horsemanship," 83.
55. Philip Morgan, "'To Get Quit of Negroes': George Washington and Slavery," *Journal of American Studies* 39, no. 3 (2005): 403–29.
56. See François Furstenberg, "Atlantic Slavery, Atlantic Freedom: George Washington, Slavery, and Transatlantic Abolitionist Networks," *The William and Mary Quarterly* 68, no. 2 (April 2011): 247–86.
57. *The Last Will and Testament of George Washington and Schedule of His Property, to Which Is Appended the Last Will and Testament of Martha Washington, Fourth Edition*, ed. John C. Fitzpatrick (Mount Vernon, VA: The Mount Vernon Ladies' Association of the Union, 1972), 4, as quoted in Thompson, "William Lee & Oney Judge," 8. Washington's will was published in Alexandria, Virginia, in January 1800, and circulated around the country in pamphlet form, so Sully could have read the text. See *The Papers of George Washington*, http://gwpapers.virginia.edu/documents/george-washingtons-last-will-and testament.
58. Jonathan M. Bryant, *Dark Places of the Earth: The Voyage of the Slave Ship Antelope* (New York: Norton, 2015), xvi–xvii.
59. Edward Biddle and Mantle Fielding, *The Life and Works of Thomas Sully, 1783–1872* (Philadelphia: Wickersham Press, 1921), 30:

"William Dunlap, journeying south in the autumn of 1819, stopped with Sully for a day or two. Of Sully, Dunlap writes: 'He was at this time painting his great picture of the crossing of the Delaware and occupied the Philosophical Hall adjoining the State House. . . . He had (built) opened an exhibition gallery with little profits.'" See also William Dunlap, *Diary of William Dunlap, 1766–1839: The Memoirs of a Dramatist, Theatrical Manager, Painter, Critic, Novelist, and Historian* (New York: New-York Historical Society, 1931), entry for October 19, 1819, 2: 473.

60. Dunlap, *Diary*, 2: 524.
61. Dunlap, *History*, 2: 273.
62. Fehl, "Thomas Sully's *Washington's Passage*," 597, 599.
63. Dunlap, *History*, 2: 273.
64. Fehl, "Thomas Sully's *Washington's Passage*," 586, and Dunlap, *Diary*, entry for April 2, 1820, 2: 524.
65. Richard C. Nylander, "Framing the Interior: The Entrepreneurial Career of John Doggett," paper presented at the Boston Furniture Forum, Winterthur Museum and Library, 2013, publication forthcoming; Georgia Brady Barnhill, "Extracts from the Journals of Ethan A. Greenwood: Portrait Painter and Museum Proprietor," *Proceedings of the American Antiquarian Society* 103, part 1 (1993): 160–61.
66. *Daily Evening Transcript*, November 4, 1846: "At the extreme end of the hall is a staircase of some twenty-five feet wide, branching off into two each of above twelve feet in width. Over these staircases hangs Sully's great picture of 'Washington Crossing the Delaware.' . . . Sully's great painting looks like a cabinet picture on the high and broad walls." As quoted in Claire McGlinchee, *The First Decade of the Boston Museum* (Boston: B. Humphries, 1940), 49–50.
67. See Harry T. Peters, *Currier & Ives: Printmakers to the American People* (Garden City, NY: Doubleday, Doran & Company, 1929), 240.
68. As quoted in Fischer, *Washington's Crossing*, 438.
69. Ibid., 1.
70. See *The Mount Vernon Ladies' Association: 150 Years of Restoring George Washington's Home* (Mount Vernon, VA: Mount Vernon Ladies' Association, February 2010).
71. *The Collector* 3, no. 16 (June 1892): 244.
72. See Geoff Edgers, "For New Wing MFA Rolls Out a Masterpiece: Moves Meticulous and Mighty Do the Trick in 11 Days," *The Boston Globe*, February 19, 2010; posted online at www.boston.com, with a video of the installation.

FIGURE ILLUSTRATIONS

pp. 6–7
Thomas Sully (American, born in England, 1783–1872)
The Passage of the Delaware, 1819
Oil on canvas, 372.1 x 525.8 cm (146½ x 207 in.)
Museum of Fine Arts, Boston
Gift of the Owners of the old Boston Museum, 03.1079

p. 12
Edward Savage (American, 1761–1817)
George Washington, 1793
Mezzotint, 45.4 x 35.2 cm (17⅞ x 13⅞ in.)
Museum of Fine Arts, Boston
The M. and M. Karolik Collection of Eighteenth-Century American Arts, 39.258

p. 15
Thomas Sully (American, born in England, 1783–1872)
Self-Portrait, 1807
Oil on panel, 43.2 x 36.2 cm (17 x 14¼ in.)
The Wadsworth Atheneum, Hartford, Connecticut
Bequest of Daniel Wadsworth, 1848.1
Photograph: Allen Phillips/Wadsworth Atheneum

p. 19
Benjamin West (American, 1738–1820)
King Lear, 1788–1806
Oil on canvas, 271.8 x 365.8 cm (107 x 144 in.)
Museum of Fine Arts, Boston
Henry H. and Zoe Oliver Sherman Fund, 1979.476

p. 20
Anthony van Dyck (Flemish, 1599–1641)
Charles the First with M. San Antoine, 1633
Oil on canvas, 370 x 270 cm (145⅝ x 106¼ in.)
Royal Collection Trust, Buckingham Palace
Royal Collection Trust/© Her Majesty Queen Elizabeth II 2015

p. 22
Jacques-Louis David (French, 1748–1825)
Napoleon Crossing the Alps, 1801
Oil on canvas, 260 x 221 cm (102⅜ x 87 in.)
Château de Malmaison et Bois-Préau
Photograph: Erich Lessing/Art Resource, NY

p. 24
Benjamin West (American, 1738–1820)
The Death of General Wolfe, 1771
Oil on canvas, 152.6 x 214.5 cm (60 x 84½ in.)
National Gallery of Canada, Ottawa
Gift of the 2nd Duke of Westminster, England, 1918; Transfer from the Canadian War Memorials, 1921
Photograph © National Gallery of Canada

p. 25
John Singleton Copley (American, 1738–1815)
The Death of Major Peirson, 1783
Oil on canvas, 251.5 x 365.8 cm (99 x 144 in.)
Tate Gallery
Photograph © 2015 Tate, London

p. 26
After Jean-Antoine Houdon (French, 1741–1828)
George Washington, probably early 19th century
Plaster cast, 22.9 x 20.3 x 15.4 cm (9¾ x 8¼ x 6 in.)
Museum of Fine Arts, Boston
Museum purchase, 88.655

p. 27
Jean-Antoine Houdon (French, 1741–1828)
Bust of George Washington, 1785
Terracotta, h. 44.4 cm (17½ in.)
Mount Vernon
Transferred to the Mount Vernon Ladies' Association through the generosity of John Augustine Washington III, 1860, W-369
Photograph courtesy of Mount Vernon Ladies' Association

p. 27
Giuseppe Ceracchi (Italian, 1751–1802)
George Washington, 1795
Marble, h. about 62 cm (24½ in.)
The Metropolitan Museum of Art, New York
Bequest of John L. Cadwalader, 1914, 14.58.235
www.metmuseum.org

p. 29
Charles Willson Peale (American, 1741–1827)
George Washington after the Battle of Princeton, 1779–82
Oil on canvas, 244.2 x 156 cm (96⅛ x 61⅜ in.)
Princeton University Art Museum
Bequest of Charles A. Munn, Class of 1881
Princeton University Art Museum/Art Resource, NY

p. 32
John Trumbull (American, 1756–1843)
Washington at the City of Charleston, 1792
Oil on canvas, 229.8 x 154.9 cm (90½ x 61 in.)
Charleston City Council
Courtesy of the City of Charleston, South Carolina

p. 33
Gilbert Stuart (American, 1755–1828)
Washington at Dorchester Heights, 1806
Oil on panel, 274.9 x 180.3 cm (108¼ x 71 in.)
Museum of Fine Arts, Boston
Deposited by the City of Boston, L-R 30.76a

p. 39
John Trumbull (American, 1756–1843)
Self-Portrait, 1777
Oil on canvas, 76.8 x 61.3 cm (30¼ x 24⅛ in.)
Museum of Fine Arts, Boston
Bequest of George Nixon Black, 29.791

p. 41
John Trumbull (American, 1756–1843)
George Washington, 1780
Oil on canvas, 91.4 x 71.1 cm (36 x 28 in.)
The Metropolitan Museum of Art, New York
Bequest of Charles Allen Munn, 1924, 24.109.88
www.metmuseum.org

p. 48
Edward Hicks (American, 1780–1849)
Passage of the Delaware after Sully, about 1840
Oil on canvas, 71.1 x 90.2 cm (28 x 35½ in.)
Chrysler Museum, Norfolk, Virginia
Gift of Edgar William and Bernice Chrysler Garbisch, 77.1271

p. 48
Emanuel Leutze (American, 1816–1868)
Washington Crossing the Delaware, 1851
Oil on canvas, 378.5 x 647.7 cm (149 x 255 in.)
The Metropolitan Museum of Art, New York
Gift of John Stewart Kennedy, 1897, 97.34
www.metmuseum.org

p. 51
The Passage of the Delaware, in original frame by John Doggett, in the Art of the Americas Wing, Museum of Fine Arts, Boston, Kristin and Roger Servison Gallery, November 10, 2010
Photograph © Museum of Fine Arts, Boston

ACKNOWLEDGMENTS

My fascination with Sully's painting began in 2001, when we set to work creating the Art of the Americas Wing, although fourteen years elapsed before I began work on this publication. For all of their inspiration and support, I especially thank my colleagues in the Art of the Americas Department: Erica Hirshler, Croll Senior Curator of American Paintings; Nonie Gadsden, Katharine Lane Weems Senior Curator of American Decorative Arts and Sculpture; Karen Quinn; Dennis Carr, Carolyn and Peter Lynch Curator of American Decorative Arts and Sculpture; Caroline Cole, Ellyn McColgan Assistant Curator of Decorative Arts and Sculpture; Taylor Poulin, Molly Richmond, and Mauri Fagan, as well as our dedicated intern, Eliza White. Sully's painting would not appear to full advantage without the extraordinary contributions of many museum professionals, especially those in Conservation and Collections Management—Rhona MacBeth, Eijk and Rose-Marie van Otterloo Conservator of Paintings; Charlotte Seifen Ameringer; Irene Konefal; Lydia Vagts, Cunningham Associate Conservator of Paintings; Jeanne Woodward, Gordon Hanlon, Andrew Haines, Frank Egloff, and Ales Hlousek—as well as Maureen Melton, Susan Morse Hilles Director of Libraries and Archives; Courtney Harris, Patrick Murphy, James Zhen, Chris Newth, and our superb Facilities crew. In MFA Publications, I am grateful to Emiko K. Usui, for her encouragement; Jennifer Snodgrass, who deftly honed the text; Terry McAweeney, who created the elegant layout based on Susan Marsh's series design; and Hope Stockton. My work on George Washington, *The Passage of the Delaware*, and Thomas Sully was generously supported by the insights of many experts, to whom I am deeply grateful, although any errors remain my own: Susan P. Schoelwer; Mary V. Thompson; David Hackett Fischer, whose book *Washington's Crossing* sets the highest standard; William Rudolph, Charles Lyle, Lorna Condon, Kimberly McCarty, Kathy Golden, Christopher Bryant, Jerry Francis, Samuel B. Webb, and Michael J. A. Darling. Heartfelt thanks to those who assisted me in myriad ways: Barbara and Ted Alfond, Lillie and Ned Johnson, Jeffrey and Jane Marshall, Anne and Greg Fields, Jamie and Phyllis Wyeth, Mary Beth Dolan, Patsy and Bobby Lawrence, Eddie and Clarke Coggeshall, Azi Djazani, Amy Poorvu, and, as always, John, William, and James Paolella. This publication is dedicated to members of the armed forces, past and present, and to the MFA's Gallery Instructors and Museum Associates, who bring Sully's painting to life.

Elliot Bostwick Davis
John Moors Cabot Chair, Art of the Americas

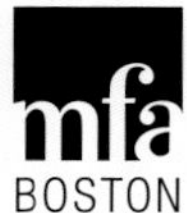

MFA Publications
Museum of Fine Arts, Boston
465 Huntington Avenue
Boston, Massachusetts 02115
www.mfa.org/publications

Generous support for this publication was provided by the Ann and William Elfers Publications Fund.

ISBN 978-0-87846-833-1

Library of Congress Control Number:2016936839

All rights reserved. No part of this book may be reproduced in any form or by any electronic or mechanical means, including information storage

The Museum is proud to be a leader within the American museum community in sharing the objects in its collection via its website. Currently, information about more than 330,000 objects is available to the public worldwide. To learn more about the MFA's collections, including provenance, publication, and exhibition history, kindly visit www.*mfa.org/collections*.

For a complete listing of MFA publications, please contact the publisher at the above address, or call 617 369 3438.

Cover images: Thomas Sully, *The Passage of the Delaware*, 1819 (details)
All illustrations in this book were photographed by the Imaging Studios, Museum of Fine Arts, Boston, except where otherwise noted.

Edited by Jennifer Snodgrass
Design and production by Terry McAweeney
Series design by Susan Marsh
Typeset by Matt Mayerchak
Production assistance by Hope Stockton
Printed and bound at Graphicom, Verona, Italy

Distributed in the United States of America and Canada by
ARTBOOK | D.A.P.
155 Sixth Avenue
New York, New York 10013
www.artbook.com

Distributed outside the United States of America and Canada by
Thames & Hudson, Ltd.
181A High Holborn
London WC1V 7QX
www.thamesandhudson.com

FIRST EDITION
Printed and bound in Italy
This book was printed on acid-free paper.